Signature

Legendary African American Distinctive Signatures
(sig'ne-cher) noun. The act of signing one's name, or distinctive mark.

Edited, Published and Compiled
Rubin Benson Bashir

First Impressions Design

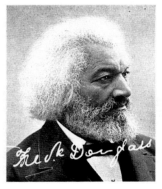

Published by First Impressions Group Inc.
Philadelphia, Pennsylvania 19143, USA
Copyright © 2018 First Impressions, Inc,
All rights reserved.

ISBN: 978 1737709213
Library of Congress Control Number: 2018968318

THIS BOOK WAS CREATED BY
Rubin Benson Bashir for First Impression Design Group, Inc. / Philadelphia PA

Book Designed and Compiled by
Rubin Benson Bashir

Photographs are © their respective owners

FIRST EDITION

First Impressions: 215.472.1660
www.firstimpressionsbooks.com

Legendary African American Distinctive Signatures

Signature

CONTENTS

Signature

C O N T E N T S

Signature

CONTENTS

Legendary African American Distinctive Signatures

Signature
CONTENTS

Signature

THE AUTHOR

Rubin A. Benson Bashir is an award-winning creative director, recognized for his exceptional talent to translate ideas into holistic visual interpretations. Partial list of his awards and honors include: Communication of Excellence to Black Audiences-CEBA Award of Excellence (1985 Album Jacket Design Award), The World Institute of Black Communications, Organization of Black Designers, Washington, D.C. (1990 Graphic Design Award), National Black Chamber of Commerce (NBCC), National Urban League (1995 Urban Advertising Design Award), CEBA Awards Panel Judge (1978-1992)

For nearly 50 years, he's worked with numerous high-profile clients including Philadelphia International Records, Philadelphia Art Museum, Philadelphia Dance Company, Mann Music Centre for Performing Arts, The National Black Music Association, CBS Records, MasterCard International, World Affairs Council, Congressional Black Caucus, Universal Companies, Bank of America, and many others. In addition, he previously worked for several advertising agencies including Benton & Bowles Advertising, Ogilvy & Mather, J. Walter Thompson Advertising, UniWorld Group, Black Enterprise Magazine, and the National Black Network.

As the creative director, he manages projects from concept to delivery and every aspect in between. An avid collector of original African-American fine art and memorabilia. This thirst gave focus to recognizing and authenticating various African-American signatures. Curious to find as many as he could have led to what is being shown in this book. This process has taken well over three years. We hope you enjoy the following pages.

Signature

INTRODUCTION

In the year 1830, the state of North Carolina adopted into law the act to prevent all persons from teaching slaves to read or write. The teaching of slaves to read or write, has a tendency to excite dissatisfaction in the minds of slaves, and will produce insurrection and rebellion, to the manifest injury of citizens of this state of North Carolina.

Any free person, who shall hereafter teach, or attempt to teach, any slave within the state to read or write or give or sell to such slave any books or pamphlets, shall be liable to indictment in any court of record in this State of North Carolina. And the slave shall be imprisoned; and or whipped at the discretion of the court, not exceeding 39 lashes and not less than 20 lashes. "Act Passed" by the General Assembly of the State of North Carolina at the Session of 1830 (Raleigh:1830).

Despite the racism of North Carolina and other united states in America, slaves did learn to read and write. Even though many slaves were not literate they would sign documents using ascribed "X" in lieu of a signature. The courts permitted this as long as the X-mark was witnessed.

The individual signatures enclosed in this unique presentation is not a critique of their "penmanship". On the contrary, our intention is only to show an individual's style of "handwriting" their name. Iconic as these African-Americans are, their signatures reveal a vibrant brand attached to their personality.

The challenge here at First Impressions was a simple one. Collect through research as many handwritten reproductions of "Famous Black folks" as could be possible. Needless to say this goal was not all that simplistic. It has taken close to three years before the collection of signature was ready to be published

In the following page we hope to show the beauty and distinctive identity of the many individuals found in our table of contents. Make no mistake this can be used a equal to their own personal finger print.

The type font displayed under all individual photographs is a digitized replica of the world famous psychoanalysis and neurologist **Sigmund Freud's** handwriting. Freud once said that there is a psychological connection of how one writes their name. And if one would analysis how a name is written you would learn much about that individual.

Type Font Compiled and Digitized by: Typographer: Herald Geisler / Germany

Alexander Miles

Born 1838, Duluth, Minnesota. Before Miles' innovations to the elevator industry, riders were required to open and close the elevator and shaft doors manually. This obviously led to many accidents, as patrons would often forget to close shaft doors and people sometimes fell to serious injury or death.

In 1887, Miles filed a patent that would automate the elevator door process; the elevator doors would operate through a series of levers and rollers, while the shaft doors would open and close with a flexible belt attached to the elevator cage. The shaft doors would open and close automatically when the belt came in contact with drum devices fixed just above and below the doors, dramatically improving elevator safety.

Alexander Murray Palmer Haley was an American writer and the author of the 1976 book Roots: The Saga of an American Family. ABC adapted the book as a television miniseries of the same name and aired it in 1977 to a record-breaking audience of 130 million viewers. In the United States the book and miniseries raised the public awareness of African American history and inspired a broad interest in genealogy and family history.

Alex Haley

Althea Gibson

Althea Gibson was an American tennis player and professional golfer, and the first black athlete to cross the color line of international tennis. In 1956, she became the first person of color to win a Grand Slam title. The following year she won both Wimbledon and the U.S. Nationals, then won both again in 1958, and was voted Female Athlete of the Year by the Associated Press in both years. In all, she won 11 Grand Slam tournaments, including six doubles titles, and was inducted into the International Tennis Hall of Fame and the International Women's Sports Hall of Fame. "She is one of the greatest players who ever lived. In the early 1960s she also became the first black player to compete on the women's professional golf tour.

Amiri Baraka (born Everett LeRoi Jones; October 7, 1934 – January 9, 2014), previously known as LeRoi Jones and Imamu Amear Baraka,was an African-American writer of poetry, drama, fiction, essays and music criticism. He was the author of numerous books of poetry and taught at several universities, including the State University of New York at Buffalo and the State University of New York at Stony Brook. He received the PEN/Beyond Margins Award, in 2008 for Tales of the Out and the Gone. Baraka's career spanned nearly 50 years, and his themes range from black liberation to white racism. Some poems that are always associated with him are "The Music: Reflection on Jazz and Blues", "The Book of Monk", and "New Music, New Poetry". Baraka's poetry and writing have attracted both high praise and condemnation.

Alvin
Ailey
1974

American radio and television sitcom set in Harlem, Manhattan's historic black community. The original radio show, which was popular from 1928 until 1960, was created, written and voiced by two white actors, When the show moved to television, black actors took over the majority of the roles.

Alvin Childress as "Amos" and Spencer Williams as "Andy" Amos 'n' Andy began as one of the first radio comedy series. After the first broadcast in 1928, the show became a hugely popular radio series. The show ran as a nightly radio serial (1928–43), as a weekly situation comedy (1943–55) and as a nightly disc-jockey program (1954–60). A television adaptation ran on CBS (1951–53) and continued in syndicated reruns (1954–66). It would not be shown to a nationwide audience again until 2012

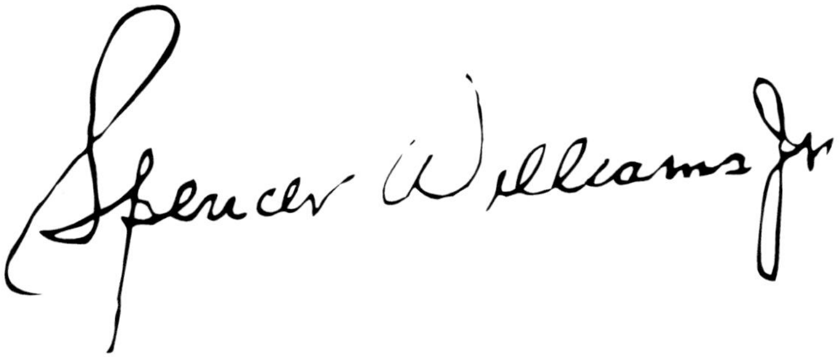

Alvin Childress

Spencer Williams Jr

Andrew Jackson Young Jr. is an American politician, diplomat, and activist. Beginning his career as a pastor, Young was an early leader in the Civil Rights Movement, serving as executive director of the Southern Christian Leadership Conference and a close confidant to Martin Luther King Jr. Young later became active in politics, serving first as a U.S. Congressman from Georgia, then United States Ambassador to the United Nations, and finally Mayor of Atlanta. Since leaving political office, Young has founded or served in a large number of organizations working on issues of public policy and political lobbying.

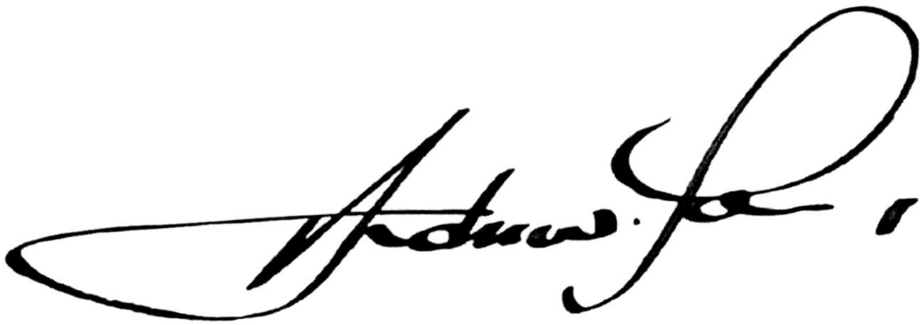

Angela Bassett

Angela Evelyn Bassett is an American actress and activist. She is best known for her biographical film roles, most notably her performance as Tina Turner in the biopic What's Love Got to Do with It, for which she was nominated for the Academy Award for Best Actress and won a corresponding Golden Globe Award. Bassett has additionally portrayed Betty Shabazz in both Malcolm X and Panther, Katherine Jackson in The Jacksons: An American Dream, Rosa Parks in The Rosa Parks Story, Voletta Wallace in Notorious and Coretta Scott King in Betty & Coretta. Bassett's performance as Parks was honored with her first Primetime Emmy Award nomination.

Angela Davis

Born in Birmingham, Alabama. She grew up in a middle class neighborhood dubbed "Dynamite Hill," due to many of the African-American homes in the area that were bombed by the Ku Klux Klan. Davis is best known as a radical African-American educator and activist for civil rights and other social issues. She knew about racial prejudice from her experiences with discrimination growing up in Alabama. As a teenager, Davis organized interracial study groups, which were broken up by the police. An American political activist, academic, and author. She emerged as a prominent counterculture activist and radical in the 1960s as a leader of the Communist Party USA, and had close relations with the Black Panther Party through her involvement in the Civil Rights Movement.

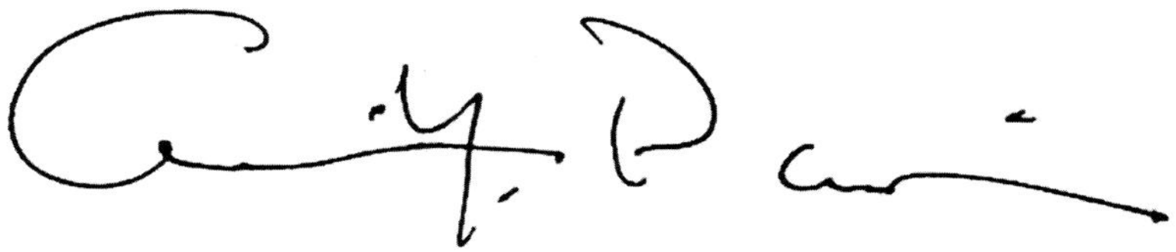

Arthur Ashe

Arthur Ashe grew up in segregated Richmond, Virgina where he decided to make a career out of tennis where he won his first U.S. Open in 1968, the first ever won by a black player. Ashe firmly established his stardom in 1975 after beating Jimmy Connors to take the Wimbledon title. As a tennis professional, he won three Grand Slam singles titles and led the U.S. to four Davis Cup victories. Over his career he won 33 singles tournaments on five continents. A sudden heart attack in 1979 ended his playing career where he underwent quadruple bypass surgery and then double bypass surgery in 1983 where he contracted AIDS from tainted blood during the surgery. Ashe kept his illness a secret until a newspaper leaked the story in early 1992 where he finally admitted that he had AIDS and became an outspoken advocate for more research.

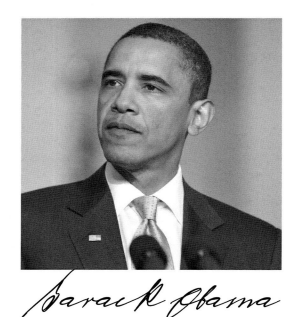

Barack Hussein Obama II is an American politician who served as the 44th President of the United States from 2009 to 2017. The first African American to assume the presidency, he was previously the junior United States Senator from Illinois from 2005 to 2008. He served in the Illinois State Senate from 1997 until 2004. On November 4, 2008, Barack Obama was elected the 44th President of the United States, winning more votes than any candidate in history. He took office at a moment of crisis unlike any America had seen in decades – a nation at war, a planet in peril, the American Dream itself threatened by the worst economic calamity since the Great Depression. And yet, despite all manner of political obstruction, Obama's leadership helped rescue the economy.

Riley B. King, known professionally as B.B. King, was an American blues singer, electric guitarist, songwriter, and record producer. King introduced a sophisticated style of soloing based on fluid string bending and shimmering vibrato that influenced many later electric blues guitarists. Rolling Stone ranked King No. 6 on its 2011 list of the 100 greatest guitarists of all time. B.B.'s first big break came in 1948 when he performed on Sonny Boy Williamson's radio program on KWEM out of West Memphis. This led to steady engagements at the Sixteenth Avenue Grill in West Memphis, and later to a ten-minute spot on black-staffed and managed Memphis radio station WDIA. "King's Spot," became so popular, it was expanded and became the "Sepia Swing Club." Soon B.B. needed a catchy radio name. Blues Boy was shortened B.B. King.

Benjamin Solomon Carson Sr. (born September 18, 1951) is an American politician, author and former neurosurgeon serving as the 17th and current United States Secretary of Housing and Urban Development since 2017, under the Trump Administration. Prior to his cabinet position, he was a candidate for President of the United States in the Republican primaries in 2016.

Born in Detroit, Michigan, and a graduate of Yale University and the University of Michigan Medical School, Carson has authored numerous books on his medical career and political stances. He was the subject of a television drama film in 2009. He was the Director of Pediatric Neurosurgery at Johns Hopkins Hospital in Maryland from 1984 until his retirement in 2013. As a pioneer in neurosurgery, Carson's achievements include performing the only successful separation of conjoined twins joined at the back of the head, pioneering the first successful neurosurgical procedure on a fetus inside the womb, performing the first completely successful separation of type-2 vertical craniopagus twins, developing new methods to treat brain-stem tumors, and reviving hemispherectomy techniques for controlling seizures. He became the youngest Chief of Pediatric Neurosurgery in the country at age 33. He has received more than 60 honorary doctorate degrees, dozens of national merit citations, and written over 100 neurosurgical publications. In 2008, he was bestowed the Presidential Medal of Freedom, the highest civilian award in the United States. On March 2, 2017, Carson was confirmed by the United States Senate as the Secretary of Housing and Urban Development in a 58–41 vote.

Benjamin Oliver Davis Jr. was an American United States Air Force general and commander of the World War II Tuskegee Airmen. He was the first African-American general officer in the United States Air Force. On December 9, 1998, he was advanced to four-star general by President Bill Clinton. During World War II, Davis was commander of the 99th Fighter Squadron and the 332nd Fighter Group, which escorted bombers on air combat missions over Europe. Davis flew sixty missions in P-39, Curtiss P-40, P-47 and P-51 Mustang fighters. Davis followed in his father's footsteps in breaking racial barriers, as Benjamin O. Davis Sr. was the first African-American general in the United States Army.

B.O. Davis Jr.
USAF

Benjamin Robinson Jr.

Born September 24, 1942 in Philadelphia, after high school Ben developed a passion for photography, and worked as a lab technician for Eastman Kodak as a photo finisher. His love for photography pushed him to establish himself as a professional photographer. Haven graduated with famed record producer and writer Kenny Gamble, Ben set out to photograph the many singing performers that were produced by the duo of Gamble & Huff. As house photographer his talent showed itself in his famed "double exposers". His reputation began to explode and Philadelphia. Not unlike James Van Der Zee of Harlem, New York City, Ben became the go-to African-American Photographer in the city of Philadelphia. He passed on September 19, 1996.

Ben Robinson

Bessie Colman

Bessie Coleman was an American civil aviatrix. She was the first woman of African-American descent and the first of Native American descent, to hold a pilot license. She achieved her international pilot license in 1921. Born to a family of sharecroppers in Texas, she went into the cotton fields at a young age but also studied in a small segregated school and went on to attend one term of college at Langston University. She developed an early interest in flying, but African Americans, Native Americans, and women had no flight-school opportunities in the United States, so she saved up money to go to France to become a licensed pilot. She soon became a successful air show pilot in the United States, and hoped to start a school for African-American fliers. She died in a plane crash in 1926 while testing her new aircraft.

Bessie Coleman

Beyoncé Knowles

Beyoncé Giselle Knowles-Carter is an American singer, songwriter and actress. Born and raised in Houston, Texas, Beyoncé performed in various singing and dancing competitions as a child. Beyoncé rose to fame in the late 1990s as lead singer of the R&B girl-group Destiny's Child. Managed by her father, Mathew Knowles, the group became one of the world's best-selling girl groups in history. Their hiatus saw Beyoncé's theatrical film debut in Austin Powers in Goldmember and the release of her debut album, Dangerously in Love. The album established her as a solo artist worldwide, earned five Grammy Awards, and featured the Billboard Hot 100 number one singles "Crazy in Love" and "Baby Boy".

34

Billie Holiday

Eleanora Fagan, better known as Billie Holiday, was an American jazz musician and singer-songwriter with a career spanning nearly thirty years. Nicknamed "Lady Day" by her friend and music partner Lester Young, Holiday had a seminal influence on jazz music and pop singing. Her vocal style, strongly inspired by jazz instrumentalists, pioneered a new way of manipulating phrasing and tempo. She was known for her vocal delivery and improvisational skills, which made up for her limited range and lack of formal music education.

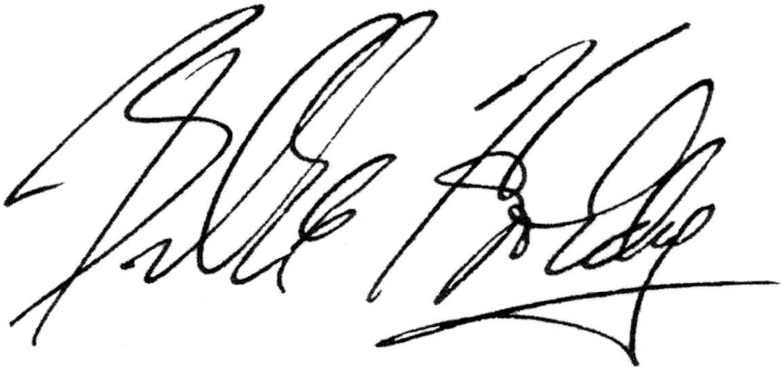

Born a slave on a Virginia farm, Washington (1856-1915) rose to become one of the most influential African-American intellectuals of the late 19th century. In 1881, he founded the Tuskegee Institute, a black school in Alabama devoted to training teachers. Washington was also behind the formation of the National Negro Business League 20 years later, and he served as an adviser to Presidents Theodore Roosevelt and William Howard Taft. Although Washington clashed with other black leaders such as W. E. B. Du Bois and drew criticism for his acceptance of segregation, he is recognized for his educational advancements and attempts to promote economic self-reliance among African Americans.

Booker T. Washington

Singer and band leader Cab Calloway was born in Rochester, New York, in 1907. He learned the art of scat singing before landing a regular gig at Harlem's famous Cotton Club. Following the enormous success of his song "Minnie the Moocher" (1931), Calloway became one of the most popular entertainers of the 1930s and '40s. He appeared on stage and in films before his death in 1994, at age 86, in Hockessin, Delaware. In 1930, Calloway got a gig at Harlem's famed Cotton Club. Soon, as the band leader of Cab Calloway and his Orchestra, he became a regular performer at the popular nightspot. The famous call-and-response "hi-de-hi-de-ho" chorus—improvised when he couldn't recall a lyric—became Calloway's signature phrase for the rest of his career

Cab Calloway

Charles Evers

James Charles Evers (born September 11, 1922) is an American civil rights activist and former politician. A Republican, Evers was known for his role in the Civil Rights Movement along with his younger brother Medgar Evers.He was made the National Association for the Advancement of Colored People (NAACP) State Voter Registration Chairman in 1954. After his brother's assassination in 1963, Evers took over his position as field director of the NAACP in Mississippi. As field director, Evers organized and led many demonstrations for the rights of African Americans. In 1969, Evers was named "Man of the Year" by the NAACP. In 1969, Evers was elected in Fayette, Mississippi, as the first African-American mayor in the state for 16 years. He unsuccessfully ran for governor in 1971.

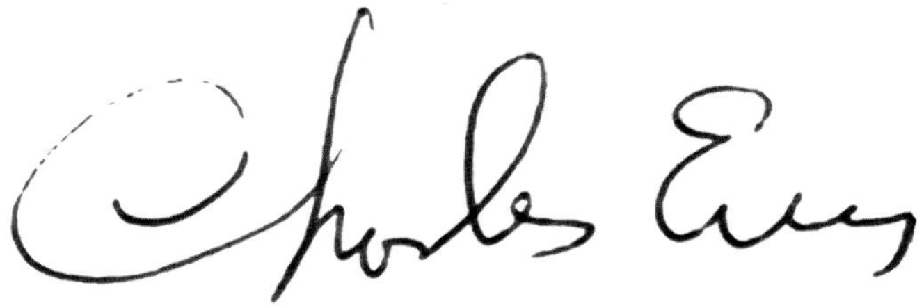

Charles Wade Barkley is an American retired professional basketball player who is currently an analyst on Inside the NBA. Nicknamed "Chuck", "Sir Charles", Barkley established himself as one of the National Basketball Association's most dominant power forwards. An All-American center at Auburn, he was drafted as a junior by the Philadelphia 76ers with the 5th pick of the 1984 NBA draft. He was selected to the All-NBA First Team five times, the All-NBA Second Team five times. He earned eleven NBA All-Star Game appearances and was named the All-Star MVP in 1991. In 1993, he was voted the league's Most Valuable Player and during the NBA's 50th anniversary, named one of the 50 Greatest Players in NBA History. In the 1992 and 1996 Olympic Games and won 2 gold medals as a member of the United States' "Dream Team".

Charlie Parker

Charles Parker Jr., also known as Yardbird and Bird, was an American jazz saxo-phonist and composer. Parker was a highly influential jazz soloist and a leading figure in the development of bebop, a form of jazz characterized by fast tempos, virtuosic technique and advanced harmonies. Parker was a blazingly fast vir-tuoso, and he introduced revolutionary harmonic ideas including rapid passing chords, new variants of altered chords, and chord substitutions. His tone ranged from clean and penetrating to sweet and somber. Parker acquired the nickname "Yardbird" early in his career. This, and the shortened form "Bird", continued to be used for the rest of his life, inspiring the titles of a number of Parker composi-tions, such as "Yardbird Suite", "Ornithology", Parker was an icon for the hipster subculture and later the Beat Generation.

Christopher Julius Rock III is an American comedian, actor, writer, producer, and director. After working as a stand-up comic and appearing in small film roles, Rock came to wider prominence as a cast member of Saturday Night Live in the early 1990s. He went on to more prominent film appearances, with starring roles in Down to Earth, Head of State, The Longest Yard, the Madagascar film series, Grown Ups, its sequel Grown Ups 2, Top Five, and a series of acclaimed comedy specials for HBO. He developed, wrote, and narrated the sitcom Everybody Hates Chris, which was based on his early life.

Cicely Tyson

Cicely Tyson was born in Harlem, New York City, where she was raised by her devoutly religious parents, from the Caribbean island of Nevis. Her mother, Theodosia, was a domestic, and her father, William Tyson, was a carpenter and painter. She was discovered by a fashion editor at Ebony magazine and, with her stunning looks, she quickly rose to the top of the modeling industry. In 1957, she began acting in Off-Broadway productions. She had small roles in feature films before she was cast as Portia in The Heart Is a Lonely Hunter (1968). Four years later, Cicely was nominated for an Academy Award for Best Actress for her sensational performance in the critically acclaimed film Sounder (1972). In 1974, she went on to portray a 110-year-old former slave in The Autobiography of Miss Jane Pittman (1974), which earned her two Emmy Awards.

Emmy Awards. She also appeared in the television mini series Roots (1977), King (1978) and A Woman Called Moses (1978). While Cicely has not appeared steadily on-screen because of her loyalty to only portray strong, positive images of Black women, she is without a doubt one of the most talented, beautiful actresses to have ever graced the stage and screen.

Cicely Tyson in 1981 married the famed trumpeter Miles Davis, their celebrated marriage lasted seven years. They divorced in 1988 the cause was irreconcilable differences.

Colin Powell

Colin Luther Powell is an American elder statesman and a retired four-star general in the United States Army. Powell was born in Harlem as the son of Jamaican immigrants. During his military career, Powell also served as National Security Advisor, as Commander of the U.S. Army Forces Command and as Chairman of the Joint Chiefs of Staff, holding the latter position during the Persian Gulf War. Powell was the first, and so far the only, African American to serve on the Joint Chiefs of Staff. He was the 65th United States Secretary of State, serving under U.S. President George W. Bush from 2001 to 2005, the first African American to serve in that position.

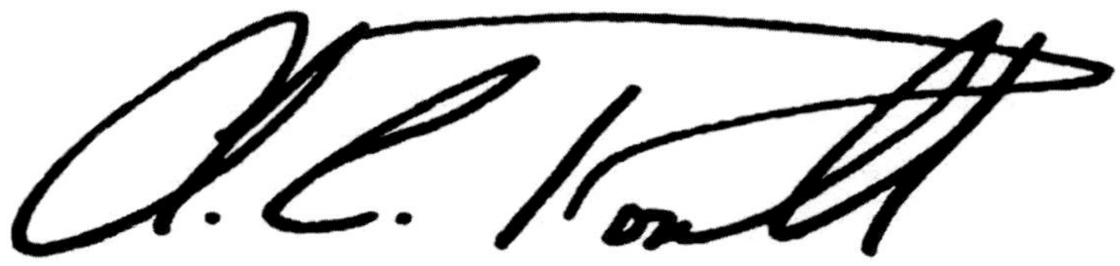

Coretta Scott King

Coretta Scott King was an American author, activist, civil rights leader, and the wife of Martin Luther King, Jr. Coretta Scott King helped lead the Civil Rights Movement in the 1960s. She was an active advocate for African-American equality. King met her husband while in college, and their participation escalated until they became central to the movement. In her early life, Coretta was an accomplished singer, and she often incorporated music into her civil rights work.

Coretta Scott King

Deborah Kaye "Debbie" Allen is an American actress, dancer, choreographer, television director, television producer, and a member of the President's Committee on the Arts and Humanities. She is perhaps best known for her work on the 1982 musical-drama television series Fame, where she portrayed dance teacher Lydia Grant, and served as the series' principal choreographer. She currently portrays Catherine Avery on Grey's Anatomy. She is the younger sister of actress/director/singer Phylicia Rashad.

Denzel Hayes Washington Jr. (born December 28, 1954) is an American actor, director, and producer. He has received three Golden Globe awards, a Tony Award, and two Academy Awards: Best Supporting Actor for the historical war drama film Glory (1989) and Best Actor for his role as a corrupt cop in the crime thriller Training Day (2001). Washington has received much critical acclaim for his film work as South African anti-apartheid activist Steve Biko in Cry Freedom (1987), Muslim minister and human rights activist Malcolm X in Malcolm X (1992), boxer Rubin "Hurricane" Carter in The Hurricane (1999), football coach Herman Boone in Remember the Titans (2000), poet and educator Melvin B. Tolson in The Great Debaters (2007), and drug kingpin Frank Lucas in American Gangster (2007).

Denzel
Washington

Diana Ernestine Earle Ross is an American singer, actress, and record producer. Born and raised in Detroit, Michigan, Ross rose to fame as the lead singer of the vocal group the Supremes, which, during the 1960s, became Motown's most successful act, and are the best charting girl group in US history, as well as one of the world's best-selling girl groups of all time. The group released a record-setting twelve number-one hit singles on the US Billboard Hot 100, including "Where Did Our Love Go", "Baby Love", "Come See About Me", "Stop! In the Name of Love", "You Can't Hurry Love", "You Keep Me Hangin' On", "Love Child", and "Someday We'll Be Together".

Diahann Carroll is an American television and stage actress, singer and model known for her performances in some of the earliest major studio films to feature black casts, including Carmen Jones and Porgy and Bess as well as on Broadway. Julia was one of the first series on American television to star a black woman in a non stereotypical role and was followed by her portrayal of Dominique Deveraux in the prime time soap opera Dynasty over three seasons. She is the recipient of numerous stage and screen nominations and awards, including the Golden Globe Award for "Best Actress In A Television Series" in 1968. She received an Academy Award for Best Actress nomination for the 1974 film Claudine. A breast cancer survivor and activist.

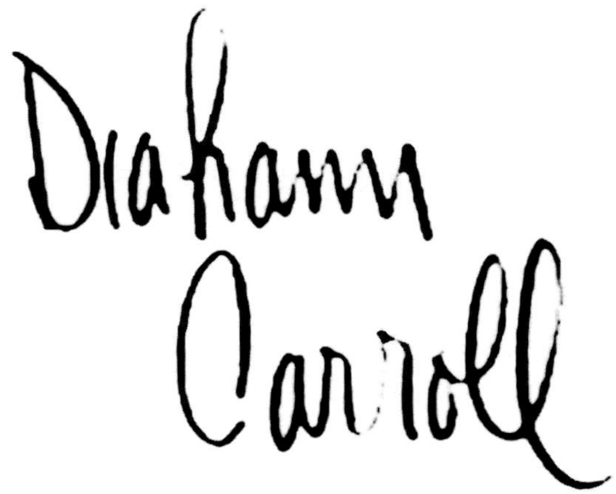
Diahann
Carroll

Dick Gregory was a pioneering comedian and civil rights activist who took on race with layered, nuanced humor during the turbulent 1960s.

Dick Gregory was born in 1932 in St. Louis, Missouri. Gregory got his big break performing as a stand-up comedian at the Playboy Club in the early 1960s. Known for his sophisticated, layered humor that took on racial issues of the day, Gregory became a comedy headliner and a trailblazer for other African-American comedians including Richard Pryor and Bill Cosby. He also participated as an activist in the Civil Rights Movement and eventually ran for political office. In his later years, he worked as a lecturer and pursued his interests in health and fitness.

Dick Gregory

Donald King (born August 20, 1931) is an American boxing promoter known for his involvement in historic boxing match ups. He has been a controversial figure, partly due to a manslaughter conviction (and later pardon), and civil cases against him. King's career highlights include, among multiple other enterprises, promoting "The Rumble in the Jungle" and the "Thrilla in Manila". King has promoted some of the most prominent names in boxing, including Muhammad Ali, Joe Frazier, George Foreman, Larry Holmes, Mike Tyson, Evander Holyfield, Julio César Chávez, Ricardo Mayorga, Andrew Golota, Bernard Hopkins, Félix Trinidad, Roy Jones Jr. and Marco Antonio Barrera. Some of these boxers sued him for allegedly defrauding them. Most of the lawsuits were settled out of court.

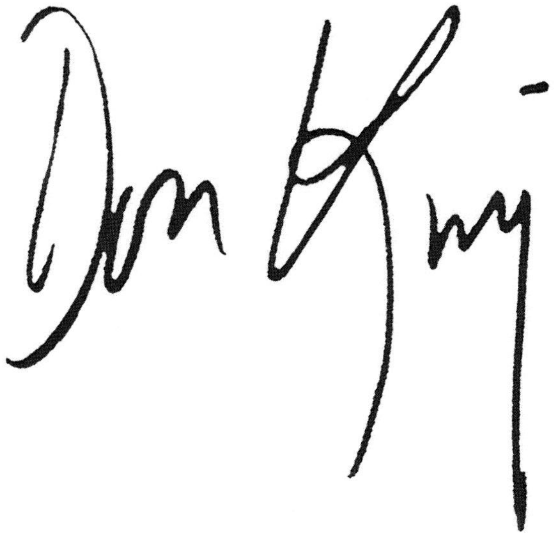

Dorothy Dandridge

Dorothy Jean Dandridge was an American film and theatre actress, singer, and dancer. She is perhaps one of the most famous African American actresses to have a successful Hollywood career and the first to be nominated for an Academy Award for Best Actress for her performance in the 1954 film Carmen Jones. Dandridge performed as a vocalist in venues such as the Cotton Club and the Apollo Theater. During her early career, she performed as a part of The Wonder Children, later The Dandridge Sisters, and appeared in a succession of films, usually in uncredited roles.

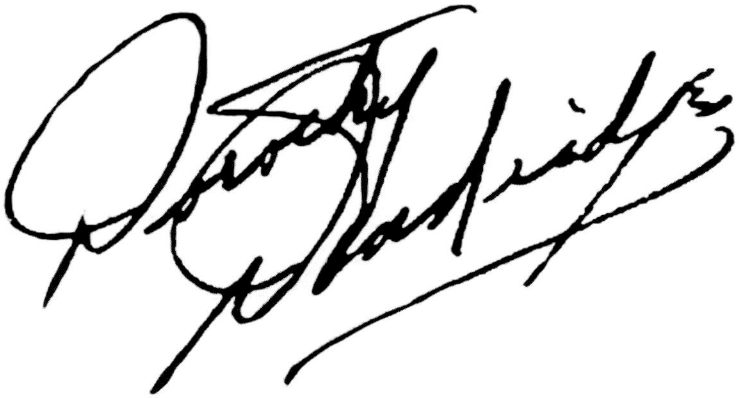

Edward Kennedy "Duke" Ellington (April 29, 1899 – May 24, 1974) was an American composer, pianist, and band leader of a jazz orchestra, which he led from
1923 until his death in a career spanning over fifty years. Born in Washington,
D.C., Ellington was based in New York City from the mid 1920s onward, and
gained a national profile through his orchestra's appearances at the Cotton Club
in Harlem. In the 1930s, his orchestra toured in Europe. Though widely considered to have been a pivotal figure in the history of jazz, Ellington embraced the
phrase "beyond category" as a liberating principle, and referred to his music as
part of the more general category of American Music. His reputation continued
to rise after he died, and he was awarded a special posthumous Pulitzer Prize for
music in 1999.

Earl Fatha Hines

Earl Kenneth Hines, universally known as Earl "Fatha" Hines (December 28, 1903 – April 22, 1983), was an American jazz pianist and band leader. He was one of the most influential figures in the development of jazz piano and, according to one major source, is "one of a small number of pianists whose playing shaped the history of jazz".]The trumpeter Dizzy Gillespie (a member of Hines's big band, along with Charlie Parker) wrote, "The piano is the basis of modern harmony. This little guy came out of Chicago, Earl Hines. He changed the style of the piano. You can find the roots of Bud Powell, Herbie Hancock, all the guys who came after that. If it hadn't been for Earl Hines blazing the path for the next generation to come. Count Basie said that Hines was, "the greatest piano player in the world".

Elijah Muhammad was born Elijah Robert Poole in Sandersville, Georgia, the seventh of thirteen children of William Poole Sr. (1868–1942), a Baptist lay preacher and sharecropper, and Mariah Hall (1873–1958), a homemaker and sharecropper. Elijah's education ended at the third grade to work in sawmills and brickyards. To support the family, he worked with his parents as a sharecropper. When he was sixteen years old, he left home and began working in factories and at other businesses. Poole married Clara Evans (1899–1972) on March 7, 1917. The Poole family was among the hundreds of thousands of black families forming the First Great Migration leaving the oppressive and economically troubled South in search of safety and employment. Poole later recounted that before the age of

20, he had witnessed the lynchings of three black men by white people. During his time as leader of the Nation of Islam, Muhammad had developed the Nation of Islam from a small movement in Detroit to an empire consisting of banks, schools, restaurants and stores across 46 cities in America. The Nation also owned over 15,000 acres of farmland, their own truck- and air- transport systems, as well as a publishing company that printed the country's largest Black newspaper. As a leader, Muhammad served as mentor to many notable members, such as Malcolm X, Muhammad Ali, Louis Farrakhan and his son Warith Deen Mohammed. The Nation of Islam is estimated to have between 20,000 and 50,000 members, and 130 mosques offering numerous social programs. Upon his death, his son Warith Deen Mohammed succeeded him.

Ethel Waters

Ethel Waters was an American singer and actress. Waters frequently performed jazz, big band, and pop music, on the Broadway stage and in concerts, but she began her career in the 1920s singing blues. Waters notable recordings include "Dinah", "Stormy Weather", "Taking a Chance on Love", "Heat Wave", "Supper Time", "Am I Blue?", "Cabin in the Sky", "I'm Coming Virginia", and her version of the spiritual "His Eye Is on the Sparrow". Waters was the second African American, after Hattie McDaniel, to be nominated for an Academy Award. She was the first African-American to star on her own television show, in 1939, and the first African-American woman to be nominated for an Emmy Award, in 1962.

Ethel Waters

Father Divine, also known as Reverend M. J. Divine, was an African American spiritual leader from about 1907 until his death. His full self-given name was Reverend Major Jealous Divine, and he was also known as "the Messenger" early in his life. He founded the International Peace Mission movement, formulated its doctrine, and oversaw its growth from a small and predominantly black congregation into a multiracial and international church.

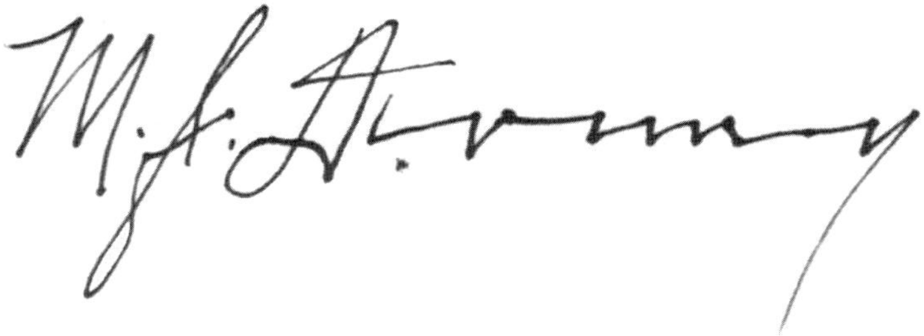

Fats Waller

Waller was the youngest of 11 children (five of whom survived childhood) born to Adeline Locket Waller, a musician, and the Reverend Edward Martin Waller in New York City. He started playing the piano when he was six and graduated to playing the organ at his father's church four years later. His mother instructed him in his youth, and he attended other music lessons, paying for them by working in a grocery store. Waller attended DeWitt Clinton High School for one semester, but left school at 15 to work as an organist at the Lincoln Theater in Harlem, where he earned $32 a week. Within 12 months he had composed his first rag. He was the prize pupil and later the friend and colleague of the stride pianist James P. Johnson. Waller's first recordings, "Muscle Shoals Blues" and "Birmingham Blues", were made in October 1922 for Okeh Records.

Fats Waller

Frederick Douglass was an African-American social reformer, abolitionist, orator, writer, and statesman. After escaping from slavery in Maryland, he became a national leader of the abolitionist movement in Massachusetts and New York, gaining note for his dazzling oratory and incisive antislavery writings. In his time, he was described by abolitionists as a living counter-example to slaveholders' arguments that slaves lacked the intellectual capacity to function as independent American citizens. Northerners at the time found it hard to believe that such a great orator had once been a slave.

Frederick Douglass

George Washington Carver

George Washington Carver, was an American botanist and inventor. He actively promoted alternative crops to cotton and methods to prevent soil depletion. While a professor at Tuskegee Institute, Carver developed techniques to improve soils depleted by repeated plantings of cotton. He wanted poor farmers to grow alternative crops, such as peanuts and sweet potatoes, as a source of their own food and to improve their quality of life. The most popular of his 44 practical bulletins for farmers contained 105 food recipes using peanuts. Although he spent years developing and promoting numerous products made from peanuts, none became commercially successful.

G. W. Carver

Guion Stewart Bluford Jr., Ph.D.,, is an American aerospace engineer, retired U.S. Air Force officer and fighter pilot, and former NASA astronaut, who was the first African American in space. Before becoming an astronaut, he was an officer in the U.S. Air Force, where he remained while assigned to NASA, rising to the rank of Colonel. He participated in four Space Shuttle flights between 1983 and 1992. In 1983, as a member of the crew of the Orbiter Challenger on the mission STS-8, he became the first African American in space as well as the second person of African ancestry in space, after Cuban cosmonaut Arnaldo Tamayo Méndez.

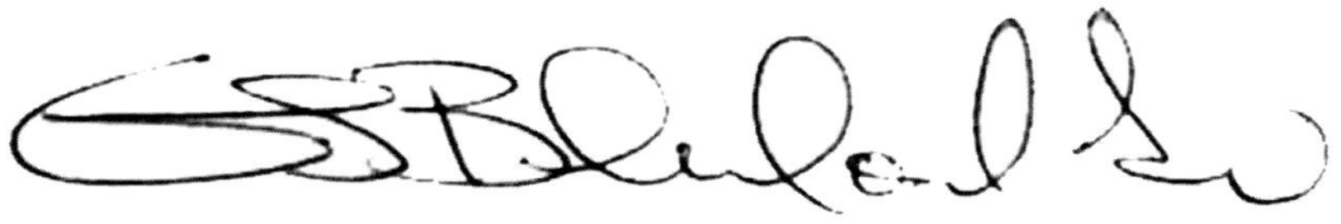

Halle Berry

Halle Maria Berry (born Maria Halle Berry; August 14, 1966) is an American actress. Berry won the 2002 Academy Award for Best Actress for her performance in the romantic drama Monster's Ball (2001). As of 2018, she is the only black woman to have won the award. Berry was one of the highest-paid actresses in Hollywood during the 2000s and has been involved in the production of several of the films in which she performed. Berry is also a Revlon spokes model. Before becoming an actress, she started modelling and entered several beauty contests, finishing as the 1st runner-up in the Miss USA Pageant and coming in 6th place in the Miss World Pageant in 1986. Her breakthrough film role was in the romantic comedy Boomerang (1992), alongside Eddie Murphy.

In a television film Introducing Dorothy Dandridge (1999), she won the Prime-time Emmy Award and Golden Globe Award for Best Actress in a Miniseries or Movie. In addition to her Academy Award win, Berry garnered high-profile roles in the 2000s, such as Storm in X-Men (2000), the action crime thriller Swordfish (2001), and the spy film Die Another Day (2002), where she played Bond Girl Jinx. She then appeared in the X-Men sequels, X2 (2003) and X-Men: The Last Stand (2006). In the 2010s, she appeared in movies such as the science fiction film Cloud Atlas (2012), the crime thriller The Call (2013) and X-Men: Days of Future Past (2014). Berry was formerly married to baseball player David Justice, and singer-songwriter Eric Benét. She has two children: a daughter fathered by model Gabriel Aubry, and a son with actor Olivier Martinez.

Henry Louis Aaron, nicknamed "Hammer" or "Hammerin' Hank", is a retired American Major League Baseball right fielder who serves as the senior vice president of the Atlanta Braves. He played 21 seasons for the Milwaukee/Atlanta Braves in the National League and two seasons for the Milwaukee Brewers in the American League, from 1954 through 1976. Aaron held the MLB record for career home runs for 33 years, and he still holds several MLB offensive records. He hit 24 or more home runs every year from 1955 through 1973, and is one of only two players to hit 30 or more home runs in a season at least fifteen times. In 1999, The Sporting News ranked Aaron fifth on its "100 Greatest Baseball Players" list.

Hank Aaron

Harry Belafonte is an American singer, songwriter, actor, and social activist. One of the most successful Jamaican-American pop stars in history, he was dubbed the "King of Calypso" for popularizing the Caribbean musical style with an international audience in the 1950s. His breakthrough album Calypso is the first million-selling LP by a single artist. Belafonte is perhaps best known for singing "The Banana Boat Song", with its signature lyric "Day-O". He has recorded in many genres, including blues, folk, gospel, show tunes, and American standards. He has also starred in several films, most notably in Otto Preminger's hit musical Carmen Jones, Island in the Sun, and Robert Wise's Odds Against Tomorrow.

Hattie McDaniels

Hattie McDaniel was an American stage actress, professional singer-songwriter, and comedian. She is best known for her role as "Mammy" in Gone with the Wind, for which she won the Academy Award for Best Supporting Actress, the first Academy Award won by an African American entertainer.

Hattie McDaniel

Henry Highland Garnet was an African-American abolitionist born circa December 23, 1815, in Kent County, Maryland. Born as a slave, Garnet and his family escaped to New York when he was about 9 years old. In the 1840s, he became an abolitionist. His "Call to Rebellion" speech in 1843 encouraged slaves to free themselves by rising up against owners. Seen as a radical, he became a controversial figure within the abolitionist movement. In 1865, Garnet became the first black speaker to preach a sermon in the House of Representatives. In 1881, he was appointed United States Minister and Counsel General (a position equivalent to ambassador today) in Liberia, and died there a few months later, on February 13, 1882.

Henry Highland Garnet

Henry O. Tanner

Henry Ossawa Tanner was an American artist and the first African-American painter to gain international acclaim. Tanner moved to Paris, France, in 1891 to study, and continued to live there after being accepted in French artistic circles. His painting entitled Daniel in the Lions' Den was accepted into the 1896 Salon, the official art exhibition of the Académie des Beaux-Arts in Paris.

Tanner was born in Pittsburgh, Pennsylvania, the first of seven children. His middle name commemorated the struggle at Osawatomie between pro- and anti-slavery partisans. His father Benjamin Tucker Tanner (1835-1923) was a bishop in the African Methodist Episcopal Church, the first independent black denomination in the United States. Being educated at Avery College and Western Theological Seminary in Pittsburgh, he developed a literary career.

In addtion, he was a political activist. His mother Sarah Tanner was born into slavery in Virginia but had escaped to the North via the Underground Railroad. She was mixed race, and Tanner himself was either a quadroon or an octoroon. The family moved to Philadelphia when Tanner was young. There his father became a friend of Frederick Douglass, sometimes supporting him, sometimes criticizing.

Herbie Hancock

Herbert Jeffrey "Herbie" Hancock is an American pianist, keyboardist, band leader, composer and actor. Starting his career with Donald Byrd, he shortly thereafter joined the Miles Davis Quintet where Hancock helped to redefine the role of a jazz rhythm section and was one of the primary architects of the post-bop sound. Hancock's music is often melodic and accessible; he has had many songs "cross over" and achieve success among pop audiences.

Herbie Hancock

Jack Roosevelt Robinson was an American professional baseball second base-man who became the first African American to play in Major League Baseball in the modern era. Robinson broke the baseball color line when the Brooklyn Dodgers started him at first base on April 15, 1947. When the Dodgers signed Robinson, they heralded the end of racial segregation in professional baseball that had relegated black players to the Negro leagues since the 1880s. Robinson was inducted into the Baseball Hall of Fame in 1962.

Jackie Robinson

James Arthur "Jimmy" Baldwin was an American novelist and social critic. His essays, as collected in Notes of a Native Son, explore palpable yet unspoken intricacies of racial, sexual, and class distinctions in Western societies, most notably in mid 20th century America. Some of Baldwin's essays are book-length, including The Fire Next Time, No Name in the Street, and The Devil Finds Work. An unfinished manuscript, Remember This House, was expanded and adapted for cinema as the Academy Award-nominated documentary film I Am Not Your Negro.

James Baldwin

James Joseph Brown was an American singer, songwriter, dancer, musician, record producer and band leader. A progenitor of funk music and a major figure of 20th century popular music and dance, he is often referred to as the "Godfather of Soul". In a career that lasted 50 years, he influenced the development of several music genres. Brown began his career as a gospel singer in Toccoa, Georgia. He joined an R&B vocal group, the Gospel Starlighters (which later evolved into the Flames) founded by Bobby Byrd, in which he was the lead singer. First coming to national public attention in the late 1950s as a member of the singing group The Famous Flames with the hit ballads "Please, Please, Please" and "Try Me", Brown built a reputation as a tireless live performer with the Famous Flames and his backing band, sometimes known as the James Brown Band or the James Brown Orchestra. His success peaked in the 1960s with the live album Live at the Apollo and hit singles such as "Papa's Got a Brand New Bag", "I Got You (I Feel Good)" and "It's a Man's Man's Man's World". During the late 1960s he moved from a continuum of blues and gospel-based forms and styles to a profoundly "Africanized" approach to music-making that influenced the development of funk music. By the early 1970s, Brown had fully established the funk sound after the formation of the J.B.s with records such as "Get Up (I Feel Like Being a) Sex Machine" and "The Payback". He also became noted for songs of social commentary, including the 1968 hit "Say It Loud – I'm Black and I'm Proud". Brown continued to perform and record until his death from pneumonia in 2006.

Shawn Corey Carter known professionally as Jay-Z, is an American rapper and businessman. He is one of the best-selling musicians of all time, having sold more than 50 million albums and 75 million singles worldwide, while receiving 21 Grammy Awards for his music. MTV ranked him the "Greatest MC of all time" in 2006. Rolling Stone ranked three of his albums—Reasonable Doubt, The Blueprint, and The Black Album—among The 500 Greatest Albums of All Time. In 2018, Forbes estimated his net worth at $900 million, making him the richest hip hop artist in the world.

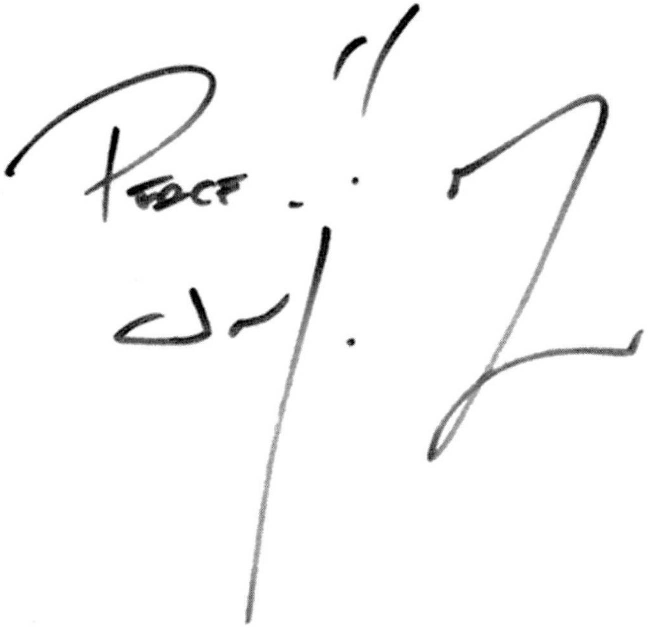

Jesse Louis Jackson Sr. is an American civil rights activist, Baptist minister, and politician. He was a candidate for the Democratic presidential nomination in 1984 and 1988 and served as a shadow U.S. Senator for the District of Columbia from 1991 to 1997. Jackson has been known for commanding public attention since he first started working for Martin Luther King Jr. In 1965, Jackson participated in the Selma to Montgomery marches organized by James Bevel, King and other civil rights leaders in Alabama. Impressed by Jackson's drive and organizational abilities, King soon began giving Jackson a role in the Southern Christian Leadership Conference (SCLC), though he was concerned about Jackson's apparent ambition and attention-seeking. When Jackson returned from Selma, he was charged with establishing a frontline office for the SCLC in Chicago. In 1966, King and Bevel selected Jackson to head the Chicago branch of the SCLC's economic arm, Operation Breadbasket and he was promoted to national director in 1967. Operation Breadbasket had been started by the Atlanta leadership of the SCLC as a job placement agency for blacks. Under Jackson's leadership, a key goal was to encourage massive boycotts by black consumers as a means to pressure white-owned businesses to hire blacks and to purchase goods and services from black-owned firms. Jackson became involved in SCLC leadership disputes following the assassination of King on April 4, 1968. When King was shot, Jackson was in the parking lot one floor below. Jackson told reporters he was the last person to speak to King, and that King died in his arms.

Jessie Owens

James Cleveland "Jesse" Owens was an American track and field athlete and four-time Olympic gold medallist in the 1936 Games. Owens specialized in the sprints and the long jump and was recognized in his lifetime as "perhaps the greatest and most famous athlete in track and field history". His achievement of setting three world records and tying another in less than an hour at the 1935 Big Ten track meet in Ann Arbor, Michigan, has been called "the greatest 45 minutes ever in sport" and has never been equalled. At the 1936 Summer Olympics in Berlin, Germany, Owens achieved international fame by winning four gold medals: 100 meters, 200 meters, long jump, and 4 × 100 meter relay. He was the most successful athlete at the Games.

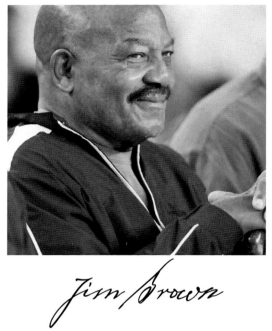

Jim Brown

James Nathaniel Brown is a former professional American football player and actor. He was a fullback for the Cleveland Browns of the National Football League from 1957 through 1965. Considered to be among the greatest football players of all time, Brown was a Pro Bowl invitee every season he was in the league, was recognized as the AP NFL Most Valuable Player three times, and won an NFL championship with the Browns in 1964. He led the league in rushing yards in eight out of his nine seasons, and by the time he retired, he had shattered most major rushing records. In 2002, he was named by The Sporting News as the greatest professional football player ever.

Jim Brown

HOF 71

Jimi Hendrix

Widely recognized as one of the most creative and influential musicians of the 20th century, Jimi Hendrix pioneered the explosive possibilities of the electric guitar. Hendrix's innovative style of combining fuzz, feedback and controlled distortion created a new musical form. Because he was unable to read or write music, it is nothing short of remarkable that Jimi Hendrix's meteoric rise in the music took place in just four short years. His musical language continues to influence a host of modern musicians, from George Clinton to Miles Davis, and Steve Vai to Jonny Lang. James Marshall "Jimi" Hendrix was an American rock guitarist, singer, and songwriter. Although his mainstream career spanned only four years, he is widely regarded as one of the most influential electric guitarists in the history of popular music, and one of the most celebrated musicians of the 20th century. The Rock and Roll Hall of Fame describes him as "arguably the greatest instrumentalist in the history of rock music".

Joseph Louis Barrow, best known as Joe Louis and nicknamed the "Brown Bomber", was an American professional boxer who competed from 1934 to 1951. He reigned as the world heavyweight champion from 1937 to 1949, and is considered to be one of the greatest heavyweights of all time. Louis' championship reign lasted 140 consecutive months, during which he participated in 26 championship fights. The 27th fight, against Ezzard Charles in 1950, was a challenge for Charles' heavyweight title and so is not included in Louis' reign. Louis was victorious in 26 title defences, second only to Julio César Chávez with 27. In 2005, Louis was ranked as the best heavyweight of all time by the International Boxing Research Organization.

Joe Louis

John Coltrane

John William Coltrane, also known as "Trane", was an American jazz saxophon-
ist and composer. Working in the bebop and hard bop idioms early in his career,
Coltrane helped pioneer the use of modes in jazz and was later at the forefront of
free jazz. He led at least fifty recording sessions during his career, and appeared
as a sideman on many albums by other musicians, including trumpeter Miles Davis and pianist Thelonious Monk.

John Coltrane (signature)

Josephine Baker

Josephine Baker was an entertainer, activist, and French Resistance agent. Her career was centered primarily in Europe, mostly in her adopted France. During her early career she was renowned as a dancer, and was among the most celebrated performers to headline the revues of the Folies Bergère in Paris. Her performance in the revue Un Vent de Folie in 1927 caused a sensation in Paris. Her costume, consisting of only a girdle of bananas, became her most iconic image and a symbol of the Jazz Age and the 1920s.

Josephine Baker

Horace Julian Bond was an American social activist and leader in the Civil Rights Movement, politician, professor and writer. While a student at Morehouse College in Atlanta, Georgia, during the early 1960s, he helped to establish the Student Nonviolent Coordinating Committee.

Kamala Harris

Kamala Harris is the Vice President of the United States, making her the first female Vice President and first Black person and Asian to hold this position. Elected in 2020 with now President Joseph Biden.

After attending Howard University and University of California Hastings College of the Law, Kamala Harris embarked on the rise through the California legal system, emerging as state attorney general in 2010. Following the November 2016 elections, Harris became just the second African American woman to win a seat in the United States Senate. She declared her candidacy for the 2020 U.S. presidential election on Martin Luther King Jr. Day 2019 but dropped out of the race before the end of the year. In August 2020, Joseph Biden announced Harris as vice presidential running mate and after a close race, Biden and Harris were elected in November 2020.

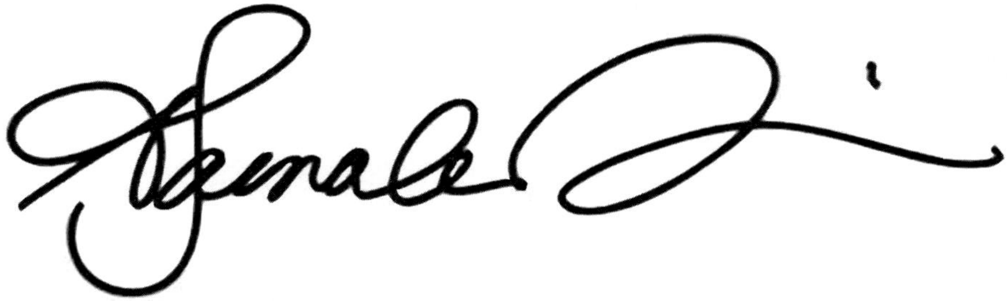

Kareem Abdul Jabbar

Kareem Abdul-Jabbar is an American retired professional basketball player who played 20 seasons in the National Basketball Association for the Milwaukee Bucks and the Los Angeles Lakers. During his career as a center, Abdul-Jabbar was a record six-time NBA Most Valuable Player, a record 19-time NBA All-Star, a 15-time All-NBA selection, and an 11-time NBA All-Defensive Team member. A member of six NBA championship teams as a player and two as an assistant coach, Abdul-Jabbar twice was voted NBA Finals MVP. In 1996, he was honored as one of the 50 Greatest Players in NBA History. NBA coach Pat Riley and players Isiah Thomas and Julius Erving have called him the greatest basketball player of all time.

Leon Huff   Kenny Gamble

In tandem with each other partners Leon Huff, producer and songwriter Kenny Gamble was the principal architect behind the lush and seductive Philly Soul sound, one of the most popular and influential musical developments of the 1970s. Born in Philadelphia on August 11, 1943, he first teamed with Huff during the late '50s while a member of the harmony group the Romeos, a unit which also included another aspiring area musician named Thom Bell, who would become crucial to Gamble's later success. "The 81," a 1964 single by the little-known Candy & the Kisses, was the inaugural Gamble-Huff co-production, and three years later the duo scored their first Top Five pop hit with the Soul Survivors' "Expressway to Your Heart." Soon recruiting the aforementioned Bell as arranger, they subsequently scored with smashes including Archie Bell & the Drells' "I Can't Stop Dancing" and Jerry Butler's "Only the Strong Survive," gradually forging their own distinctive sound. Kenny Gamble and the "Sound of Philadelphia are often compared to Barry Gordy and the "Motown Sound". But anyone who prides themselves as a connoisseur of R&B music, will quickly tell you that the music generated by the orchestration of MFSB is distinctive only to what is now called "The Sound Of Philadelphia.

Kobe Bryant   1978 • 2020

Kobe Bean Bryant is an American former professional basketball player. He played his entire 20-year career with the Los Angeles Lakers of the National Basketball Association. He entered the NBA directly from high school and won five NBA championships with the Lakers. Bryant is an 18-time All-Star, 15-time member of the All-NBA Team, and 12-time member of the All-Defensive team. He led the NBA in scoring during two seasons and ranks third on the league's all-time regular season scoring and fourth on the all-time postseason scoring list. He holds the NBA record for the most seasons playing with one franchise for an entire career and is widely regarded as one of the greatest basketball players of all time. Bryant and his daughter GiGi died in a Helicopter accident January 26, 2020.

Labron James

LeBron Raymone James is an American professional basketball player for the Cleveland Cavaliers of the National Basketball Association. Widely regarded as one of the greatest NBA players of all time, he has won three NBA championships, four NBA Most Valuable Player Awards, three NBA Finals MVP Awards, three NBA All-Star Game MVP Awards, two Olympic gold medals, an NBA scoring title, and the NBA Rookie of the Year Award. James is a 14-time NBA All-Star, 11-time All-NBA first teamer, and five-time All-Defensive first teamer. He is also the Cavaliers' all-time scoring leader, the NBA All-Star Game career scoring leader, and the NBA career playoff scoring leader.

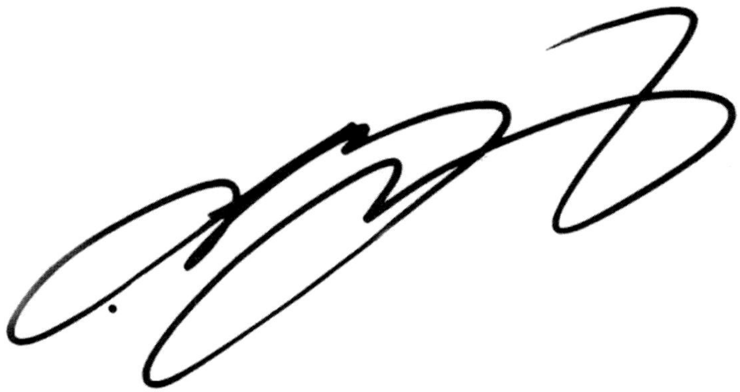

Langston Hughes

James Mercer Langston Hughes was born February 1, 1902, in Joplin, Missouri. His parents divorced when he was a young child, and his father moved to Mexico. He was raised by his grandmother until he was thirteen, when he moved to Lincoln, Illinois, to live with his mother and her husband, before the family eventually settled in Cleveland, Ohio. It was in Lincoln that Hughes began writing poetry. After graduating from high school, he spent a year in Mexico followed by a year at Columbia University in New York City. During this time, he held odd jobs such as assistant cook, launderer, and busboy. He also travelled to Africa and Europe working as a seaman. In November 1924, he moved to Washington, D. C. Hughes's first book of poetry, The Weary Blues, (Knopf, 1926) was published by Alfred A. Knopf in 1926. He finished his college education at Lincoln University in Pennsylvania three years later. In 1930 his first novel, Not Without Laughter, 1930 won the Harmon gold medal for literature.

Langston Hughes

Lena Mary Calhoun Horne was an African American singer, dancer, actress, and civil rights activist. Horne's career spanned over 70 years appearing in film, television, and theater. Horne joined the chorus of the Cotton Club at the age of 16 and became a nightclub performer before moving to Hollywood, where she had small parts in numerous movies, and more substantial parts in the 1943 films Cabin in the Sky and Stormy Weather. Because of the Red Scare and her political activism, Horne found herself blacklisted and unable to get work in Hollywood.

Lena Horne

Lewis Carl Davidson Hamilton MBE is a British racing driver who races in Formula One for the Mercedes AMG Petronas team. A four-time Formula One World Champion, he is often considered the best driver of his generation and widely regarded as one of the greatest drivers in the history of the sport. He won his first World Championship title with McLaren in 2008, then moved to Mercedes where he won back-to-back titles in 2014 and 2015 before winning his fourth title in 2017. Statistically the most successful British driver in the history of the sport, Hamilton has more World Championship titles and more race victories than any other British driver in Formula One. He also holds records for the all-time most career points, the most wins at different circuits, the all-time most pole positions and the most grand slams in a season.

Little Richard

Richard Wayne Penniman, known as Little Richard, is an American musician, songwriter, singer, and actor. An influential figure in popular music and culture for seven decades, Little Richard's most celebrated work dates from the mid-1950s, when his dynamic music and charismatic showmanship laid the foundation for rock and roll. His music also played a key role in the formation of other popular music genres, including soul and funk. Little Richard influenced numerous singers and musicians across musical genres from rock to hip hop; his music helped shape rhythm and blues for generations to come, and his performances and headline-making thrust his career right into the mix of American popular music.

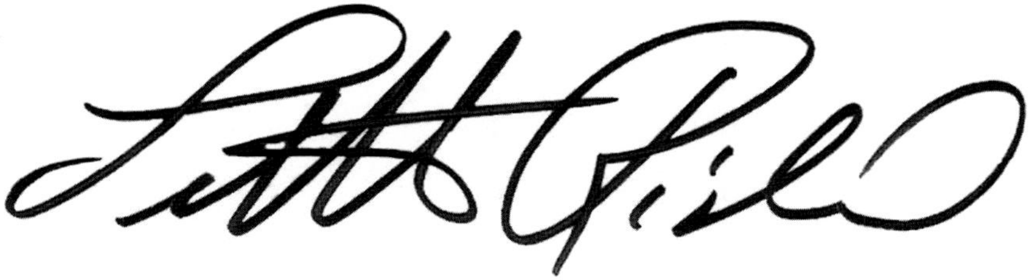

Lola Falana

Loletha Elayne Falana or Loletha Elaine Falana, better known by her stage name Lola Falana, is an American singer, dancer, model and actress. Born in Camden, New Jersey, Falana was the third of six children born to Bennett, and Cleo Falana. Falana's father, an Afro-Cuban, left his homeland of Cuba to serve in the U.S. Marine Corps. By the age of three Falana was dancing, and by age five she was singing in the church choir. In 1952, Falana's family which by this time included two more siblings, moved to Philadelphia, Pennsylvania. By the time she was in junior high school, she was already dancing in nightclubs escorted by her mother. Music became so important to her that, against her parents' wishes, Falana dropped out of Germantown High School a few months before graduation and moved to New York City.

Louis Armstrong

Louis Daniel Armstrong, nicknamed Satchmo, Satch, and Pops, was an American trumpeter, composer, singer and occasional actor who was one of the most influential figures in jazz. His career spanned five decades, from the 1920s to the 1960s, and different eras in the history of jazz. In 2017, he was inducted into the Rhythm & Blues Hall of Fame.

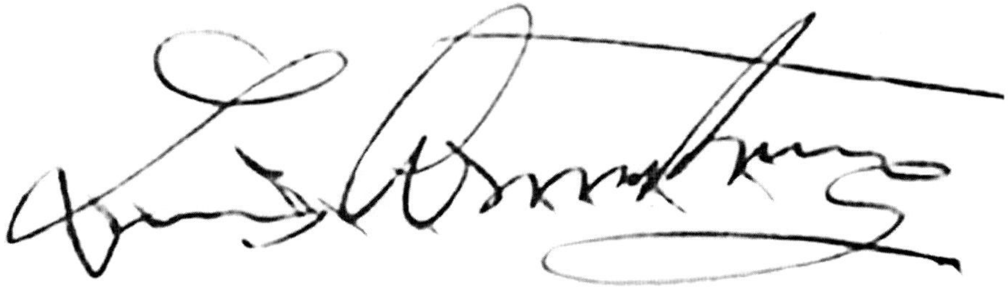

Louis Farrakhan Sr., formerly known as Louis X, is an American religious leader, African-American activist, and social commentator. He is the leader of the religious group Nation of Islam and served as the minister of major mosques in Boston and Harlem, and was appointed by longtime Nation of Islam leader the Honorable Elijah Muhammad as the National Representative of the Nation of Islam.

Louis Stokes

Lucy Eldine Gonzalez Parsons was an American labor organizer, radical socialist and anarchist communist. She is remembered as a powerful orator. Parsons
entered the radical movement following her marriage to newspaper editor Albert
Parsons and moved with him from Texas to Chicago, where she contributed to
the newspaper he famously edited—The Alarm. Following her husband's 1887
execution in conjunction with the Haymarket Affair, Parsons remained a leading
American radical activist, as a founder of the Industrial Workers of the World and
member of other political organizations.

Lucy E. Parsons

Sarah Breedlove (December 23, 1867 – May 25, 1919), known as Madam C. J. Walker, was an African-American entrepreneur, philanthropist, and a political and social activist. Eulogized as the first female self-made millionaire in America, she became one of the wealthiest African-American women in the country, "the world's most successful female entrepreneur of her time," and one of the most successful African-American business owners ever. Walker made her fortune by developing and marketing a line of beauty and hair products for black women. Madame C. J. Walker Manufacturing Company, the successful business she founded. Walker was also known for her philanthropy and activism.

Mme. C. J. Walker

Malcolm X

Malcolm X was an African-American Muslim minister and human rights activist. To his admirers he was a courageous advocate for the rights of blacks, a man who indicted white America in the harshest terms for its crimes against black Americans; detractors accused him of preaching racism and violence. He has been called one of the greatest and most influential African Americans in history. Malcolm was the national spokes person for the national organization The Nation of Islam under the leadership of the honorable Elijah Muhammad. In 1965 he separated from the Nation of Islam in a dispute with leadership. And in the same year was assassinated at the New York Audubon auditorium in Harlem.

As Salaam Alaik

Bro Malcolm X

Marcus Garvey

Marcus Mosiah Garvey Jr. ONH was a proponent of Black nationalism in Jamaica and especially the United States. He was a leader of a mass movement called Pan-Africanism and he founded the Universal Negro Improvement Association and African Communities League. He also founded the Black Star Line, a shipping and passenger line which promoted the return of the African diaspora to their ancestral lands. Although most American Black leaders condemned his methods and his support for racial segregation, Garvey attracted a large following. The Black Star Line went bankrupt and Garvey was imprisoned for mail fraud in the selling of its stock. His movement then rapidly collapsed.

Martin Luther King

Martin Luther King Jr. was an American Baptist minister and activist who became the most visible spokesperson and leader in the civil rights movement from 1954 until his death in 1968. King is best known for advancing civil rights through nonviolence and civil disobedience, tactics his Christian beliefs and the nonviolent activism of Mahatma Gandhi helped inspire. King led the 1955 Montgomery bus boycott and in 1957 became the first president of the Southern Christian Leadership Conference (SCLC). With the SCLC, he led an unsuccessful 1962 struggle against segregation in Albany, Georgia, and helped organize the nonviolent 1963 protests in Birmingham, Alabama. He also helped organize the 1963 March on Washington, where he delivered his famous "I Have a Dream" speech.

On October 14, 1964, King won the Nobel Peace Prize for combating racial inequality through nonviolent resistance. In 1965, he helped organize the Selma to Montgomery marches. The following year, he and the SCLC took the movement north to Chicago to work on segregated housing. In his final years, he expanded his focus to include opposition towards poverty and the Vietnam War. He alienated many of his liberal allies with a 1967 speech titled "Beyond Vietnam". J. Edgar Hoover considered him a radical and made him an object of the FBI from 1963 on. FBI agents investigated him for possible communist ties, recorded his extramarital liaisons and reported on them to government officials, and on one occasion mailed King a threatening anonymous letter, which he interpreted as an attempt to make him commit suicide.

In 1968, King was planning a national occupation of Washington, D.C., to be called the Poor People's Campaign, when he was assassinated on April 4 in Memphis, Tennessee.

Maya Angelou

Maya Angelou was an American poet, singer, memoirist, and civil rights activist. She published seven autobiographies, three books of essays, several books of poetry, and was credited with a list of plays, movies, and television shows spanning over 50 years. She received dozens of awards and more than 50 honorary degrees. Angelou is best known for her series of seven autobiographies, which focus on her childhood and early adult experiences. The first, I Know Why the Caged Bird Sings, tells of her life up to the age of 17 and brought her international recognition and acclaim.

Miles Davis

Miles Dewey Davis III was an American jazz trumpeter, bandleader, and composer. He is among the most influential and acclaimed figures in the history of jazz and 20th century music. Davis adopted a variety of musical directions in his five-decade career which kept him at the forefront of a number of major stylistic developments in jazz.

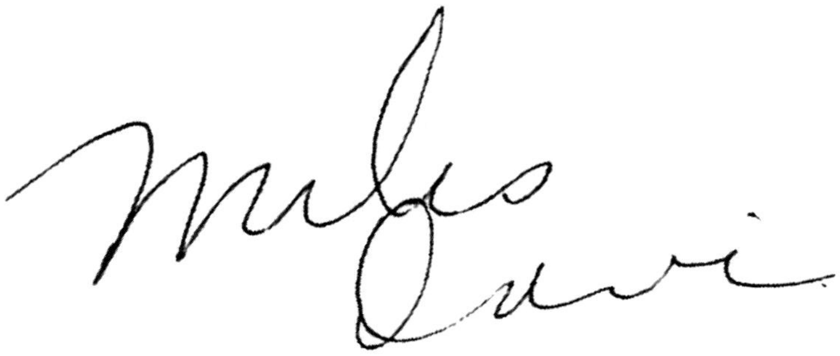

Michael Jackson

Michael Joseph Jackson was an American singer, songwriter, and dancer. Dubbed the "King of Pop", he was one of the most popular entertainers in the world, and was the best-selling music artist during the year of his death. Jackson's contributions to music, dance, and fashion along with his publicized personal life made him a global figure in popular culture for over four decades.

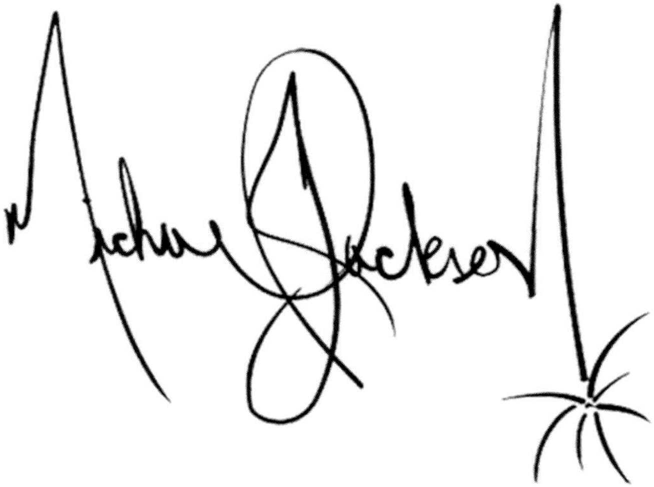

Michael Jordan

Michael Jeffrey Jordan, also known by his initials, MJ, is an American retired professional basketball player. Jordan played 15 seasons in the National Basketball Association for the Chicago Bulls and Washington Wizards. His biography on the NBA website states: "By acclamation, Michael Jordan is the greatest basketball player of all time." Jordan was one of the most effectively marketed athletes of his generation and was considered instrumental in popularizing the NBA around the world in the 1980s and 1990s. He is currently the principal owner and chairman of the NBA's Charlotte Hornets.

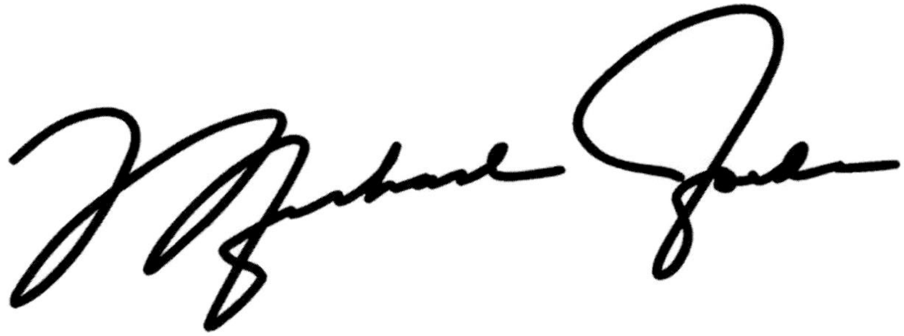

Michelle Obama

Michelle LaVaughn Robinson Obama is an American lawyer and writer who served as the First Lady of the United States from 2009 to 2017. She is married to the 44th U.S. President, Barack Obama, and was the first African-American First Lady. Raised on the South Side of Chicago, Illinois, Obama is a graduate of Princeton University and Harvard Law School, and spent her early legal career working at the law firm Sidley Austin, where she met her husband. She subsequently worked as the Associate Dean of Student Services at the University of Chicago and the Vice President for Community and External Affairs of the University of Chicago Medical Center. Barack and Michelle married in 1992 and have two daughters.

Michelle Obama

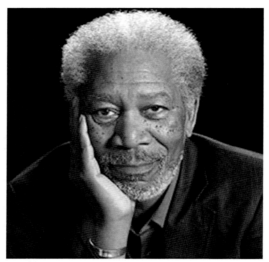

Morgan Freeman

Morgan Freeman born June 1, 1937 is an American actor, producer, and narrator. Freeman won an Academy Award in 2005 for Best Supporting Actor with Million Dollar Baby (2004), and he has received Oscar nominations for his performances in Street Smart (1987), Driving Miss Daisy (1989), The Shawshank Redemption (1994), and Invictus (2009). He has also won a Golden Globe Award and a Screen Actors Guild Award. Freeman has appeared in many other box office hits, including Glory (1989), Robin Hood: Prince of Thieves (1991), Seven (1995), Deep Impact (1998), The Sum of All Fears (2002), Bruce Almighty (2003), The Dark Knight Trilogy (2005–2012), Wanted (2008), RED (2010), Now You See Me (2013), The Lego Movie (2014), and Lucy (2014). He rose to fame as part of the cast of the 1970s children's program The Electric Company.

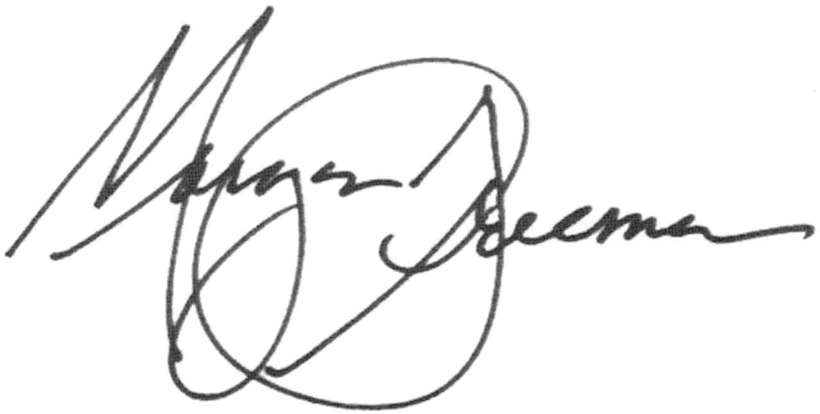

Muhammad Ali

Muhammad Ali born Cassius Marcellus Clay Jr. January 17, 1942 was an American professional boxer, activist, and philanthropist. He is widely regarded as one of the most significant and celebrated sports figures of the 20th century. From early in his career, Ali was known as an inspiring, controversial, and polarizing figure both inside and outside of the ring. He was born and raised in Louisville, Kentucky, and began training as an amateur boxer when he was 12 years old. At age 18, he won a gold medal in the light heavyweight division at the 1960 Summer Olympics in Rome, then turned professional later that year, before converting to Islam after 1961. At age 22, in 1964, he won the world heavyweight championship from Sonny Liston in a major upset. He then changed his name from Cassius Clay, which he called his "slave name", to Muhammad Ali. He set an example of racial pride for African Americans and resistance to white domination during the Civil Rights Movement. In 1966, two years after winning the heavyweight title, Ali further antagonized the white establishment by refusing to be drafted into the U.S. military, citing his religious beliefs, and opposition to American involvement in the Vietnam War. He was eventually arrested, found guilty of draft evasion charges, and stripped of his boxing titles. He successfully appealed the decision to the U.S. Supreme Court, which overturned his conviction in 1971, by which time he had not fought for nearly four years and thereby lost a period of peak performance as an athlete. Ali's actions as a conscientious objector to the war made him an icon for the larger counterculture generation. Ali was one of the leading heavyweight boxers of the 20th century, and remains the only three-time lineal champion of that division. His records of beating 21 boxers for the world heavyweight title (shared with Joe Louis). He was also ranked as the greatest athlete of the 20th century by Sports Illustrated. of the 20th century by ESPN Sports Century. Nicknamed "the Greatest".

As a Muslim, Ali was initially affiliated with Elijah Muhammad's Nation of Islam and advocated their black separatist ideology. In 1984, he was diagnosed with Parkinson's syndrome, which some reports attribute to boxing-related injuries. Ali passed on June 3rd, 2016.

Nat King Cole

Nathaniel Adams Coles, known professionally as Nat King Cole, was an American jazz pianist and vocalist. He recorded over one hundred songs that became hits on the pop charts. His trio was the model for small jazz ensembles that followed. Cole also acted in films and on television and performed on Broadway. He was the first black man to host an American television series.

Nelson Mandella

Nelson Rolihlahla Mandela was a South African anti-apartheid revolutionary, political leader, and philanthropist, who served as President of South Africa from 1994 to 1999. He was the country's first black head of state and the first elected in a fully representative democratic election. His government focused on dismantling the legacy of apartheid by tackling institutionalised racism and fostering racial reconciliation. Ideologically an African nationalist and socialist, he served as President of the African National Congress party from 1991 to 1997. He is still considered a national hero.

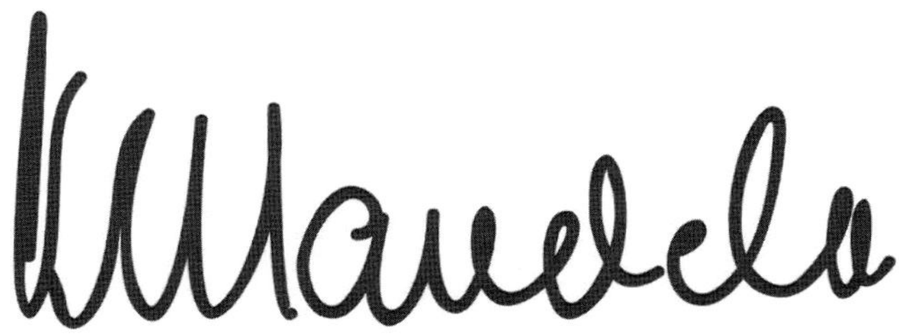

Octavius Catto

Octavius Valentine Catto was a black educator, intellectual, and civil rights activist in Philadelphia. He became principal of male students at the Institute for Colored Youth, where he had also been educated. Born free in Charleston, South Carolina, in a prominent mixed-race family, he moved north as a boy with his family. He became educated and served as a teacher, becoming active in civil rights. As a man, he also became known as a top cricket and baseball player in 19th-century Philadelphia, Pennsylvania.

Octavius V. Catto

Oprah Winfrey

Oprah Winfrey is an American media proprietor, talk show host, actress, producer, and philanthropist. She is best known for her talk show The Oprah Winfrey Show, which was the highest-rated television program of its kind in history and was nationally syndicated from 1986 to 2011 in Chicago, Illinois. Dubbed the "Queen of All Media", she was the richest African American of the 20th Century North America's first multi- billionaire black person and has been ranked the greatest black philanthropist in American history. Several assessments rank her as the most influential woman in the world.

Sean John Combs, also known by his stage names Puff Daddy, Puffy, P. Diddy and Diddy, is an American rapper, singer, songwriter, actor, record producer, and entrepreneur. He was born in New York City and was raised in Mount Vernon, New York. He worked as a talent director at Uptown Records before founding his label Bad Boy Entertainment in 1993. His debut album No Way Out has been certified seven times platinum and was followed by successful albums such as Forever, The Saga Continues..., and Press Play. In 2009, Combs formed the musical group Diddy – Dirty Money and released the critically well-reviewed and commercially successful album Last Train to Paris.

Paul Robeson

Paul Leroy Robeson was an American bass baritone concert artist and stage and film actor who became famous both for his cultural accomplishments and for his political activism. Educated at Rutgers College and Columbia University, he was also a star athlete in his youth. His political activities began with his involvement with unemployed workers and anti-imperialist students whom he met in Britain and continued with support for the Loyalist cause in the Spanish Civil War and his opposition to fascism. In the United States he also became active in the Civil Rights Movement and other social justice campaigns. His sympathies for the Soviet Union and for communism, and his criticism of the United States government and its foreign policies, caused him to be blacklisted during the McCarthy era.

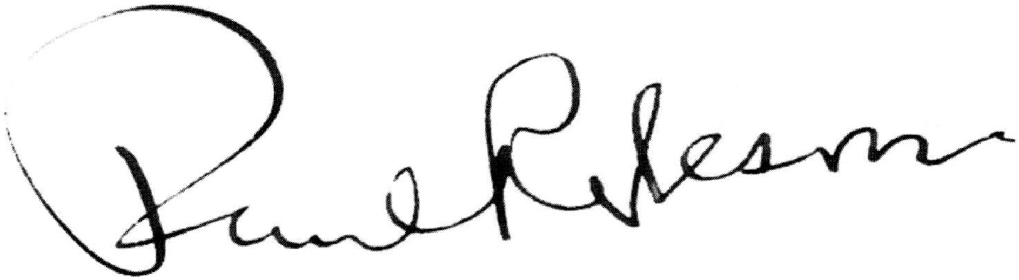

Pearl Bailey

Pearl Mae Bailey was an American actress and singer. After appearing in vaudeville she made her Broadway debut in St. Louis Woman in 1946. She won a Tony Award for the title role in the all-black production of Hello, Dolly! in 1968. In 1986, she won a Daytime Emmy award for her performance as a fairy godmother in the ABC After-school Special, Cindy Eller: A Modern Fairy Tale.

Love

Pearl Bailey

Prince Rogers Nelson was an American singer, songwriter, musician, record producer, actor, and director. Born and raised in Minneapolis, Minnesota, Prince was known for his electric work, flamboyant stage presence, extravagant fashion sense and use of makeup, and wide vocal range. His innovative music integrated a wide variety of styles, including funk, rock, R&B, new wave, soul, psychedelic, and pop. He sold over 100 million records worldwide, making him one of the best-selling music artists of all time. He won eight Grammy Awards, six American Music Awards, a Golden Globe Award, and an Academy Award for the 1984 film Purple Rain. He was inducted into the Rock and Roll Hall of Fame in 2004.

Prince Charming

Ray Charles

Ray Charles Robinson was an American singer-songwriter, musician and composer known as Ray Charles. He was a pioneer in the genre of soul music during the 1950s by fusing rhythm and blues, gospel, and blues styles into his early recordings with Atlantic Records. He also helped racially integrate country and pop music during the 1960s with his crossover success on ABC Records, most notably with his Modern Sounds albums. While with ABC, Charles became one of the first African-American musicians to be given artistic control by a mainstream record company. Frank Sinatra called Charles "the only true genius in show business," although Charles down played this notion.

RAYCHARLES

Rihanna

Robyn Rihanna Fenty is a Barbadian-born singer, songwriter, actress, and businesswoman. Born in Saint Michael, Barbados, and raised in Bridgetown, during 2003, she recorded demo tapes under the direction of record producer Evan Rogers and signed a recording contract with Def Jam Recordings after auditioning for its then-president, hip hop producer and rapper Jay-Z. In 2005, Rihanna rose to fame with the release of her debut studio album Music of the Sun and its follow-up A Girl like Me, which charted on the top 10 of the US Billboard 200 and respectively produced the successful singles "Pon de Replay", "SOS" and "Unfaithful".

Robert F. Smith

Robert Frederick Smith is an American businessman, investor and philanthropist, A former chemicaal engineer and investment banker, he is the founder, Chairman and CEO of private equity firm Vista Equity Parterners. IN 2018, Smith was ranked by Forbes as the 163rd richest person in America. He was No. 480 on Forbes 2018 list of the world's billionaires, with a net worth of US$4.4 billion. Smith was also included in Vanity Fair's New Establishment List. In 2017, Smith was named by Forbes as one of the 100 greatest living business minds. In a 2018 cover story, Forbes declared Smith the wealthest African-American, surpassing Oprah Winfrey.

R'Smith

Rosa Louise McCauley Parks was an activist in the civil rights movement best known for her pivotal role in the Montgomery Bus Boycott. The United States Congress has called her "the first lady of civil rights" and "the mother of the freedom movement". Rosa Louise McCauley Parks was an activist in the civil rights movement best known for her pivotal role in the Montgomery Bus Boycott. The United States Congress has called her "the first lady of civil rights" and "the mother of the freedom movement".

Rosa Parks

Dr. Rubin Bashir

Dr. Bashir graduated with honours from Howard University. He received his Medical Doctorate from Georgetown University School of Medicine where he also graduated with honors. He finished a five-year orthopaedic surgical residency at the University of Pittsburgh, then moved to San Francisco to complete a spinal surgery fellowship with the San Francisco Spine Institute/Spinecare Medical Group. Dr. Bashir is trained in all aspects of operative and non-operative management of degenerative spinal disease, spinal stenosis, neck and back pain, and herniated disks. He has extensive training in minimally invasive and microscopic techniques, in addition to lateral access spine surgery, and disc replacement technology. Dr. Bashir has made many scientific presentations at orthopaedic meeting and was awarded "Best Poster" presentation at a cervical spine research meeting. Dr. Bashir is a member of the American Medical Association, the J. Robert Gladden Society, and the Society of Lateral Access Surgery. Specialities: Cervical, Thoracic, Lumbar, Disc Replacement, Minimally Invasive Surgery, Microscopic Spine Surgery.

Sammy Davis Jr.

Samuel George Davis Jr. was an American singer, dancer, actor and comedian. He was noted for his impressions of actors, musicians and other celebrities. At the age of three, Davis began his career in vaudeville with his father, Sammy Davis Sr. and the Will Mastin Trio, which toured nationally. After military service, Davis returned to the trio. Davis became an overnight sensation following a nightclub performance at Ciro's after the 1951 Academy Awards. With the trio, he became a recording artist. In 1954, he lost his left eye in a car accident, and several years later, he converted to Judaism finding commonalities between the oppression experienced by African-American and Jewish communities.

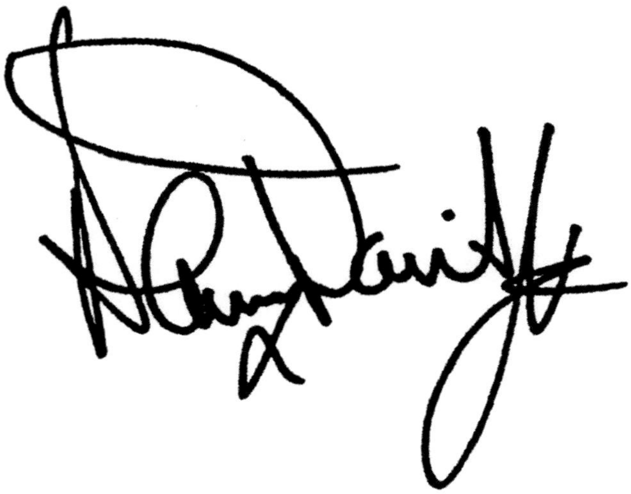

Samuel L. Jackson

Samuel Leroy Jackson is an American actor and film producer. He achieved prominence and critical acclaim in the early 1990s with films such as Goodfellas, Jungle Fever, Patriot Games, Amos & Andrew, True Romance, Jurassic Park and his collaborations with director Quentin Tarantino including Pulp Fiction, Jackie Brown, Django Unchained, and The Hateful Eight. He is a highly prolific actor, having appeared in over 100 films, including Die Hard with a Vengeance, Unbreakable, Shaft, The 51st State, Black Snake Moan, Snakes on a Plane, and the Star Wars prequel trilogy.

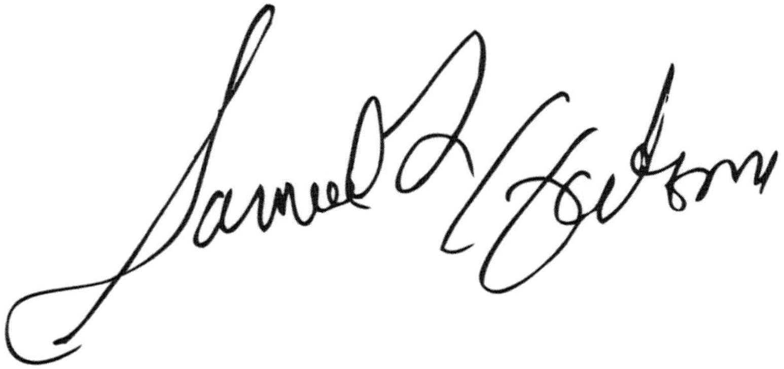

Sarah Vaughn

Sarah Lois Vaughan was an American jazz singer. She has been described by music critic Scott Yanow as having "one of the most wondrous voices of the 20th century." Nicknamed "Sassy" and "The Divine One", Vaughan was a four-time Grammy Award winner, including a "Lifetime Achievement Award". The National Endowment for the Arts bestowed upon her its "highest honor in jazz", the NEA Jazz Masters Award, in 1989.

Sarah Vaughon

Serena Williams

Serena Williams, is one of the top female tennis player in the world, has always maintained a level of interest. She earned her first grand slam singles title at the U.S. Open back in 1999, and made a string of four straight grand slam singles title wins - the 2002 French, Wimbledon, and U.S. Open titles, and the 2003 Australian Open title, all achieved by defeating her older sister, Venus. A knee injury in 2003 forced her to sit out 8 months of tennis competition. She reached the Wimbledon final in 2004, but has not won a major title since the summer of 2003. As of late, Serena has taken a stab at acting, appearing in guest roles on both The Simpsons (1989) and My Wife and Kids (2001). Serena was born in Saginaw, Michigan, to Richard and Oracene Williams (now divorced). Serena grew up with Venus and older sisters Lyndrea, Isha & Yetunde.

Shaquille Rashaun O'Neal, nicknamed "Shaq", is an American retired professional basketball player currently serving as a sports analyst on the television program Inside the NBA. He is widely considered one of the greatest players in NBA history. At 7 ft 1 in tall and 325 pounds, he was one of the heaviest players ever to play in the NBA, where he played for six teams throughout his 19-year career. Shaquille O'Neal's off-court accolades rival his athletic accomplishments, having found success in acting, music, television and gaming. Currently, Shaq is an analyst on Inside The NBA. Philanthropically, Shaquille's relationship with the Boys & Girls Club of America dates back to his youth in New Jersey. As a national spokesperson for the Boys & Girls Clubs of America, he has been participating in campaigns with the non-profit company for the past 15 years.

Shirley Chisholm

Born in Brooklyn, New York, in 1924, Shirley Chisholm is best known for becoming the first black congresswoman (1968), representing New York State in the U.S. House of Representatives for seven terms. She went on to run for the 1972 Democratic nomination for the presidency—becoming the first major-party African-American candidate to do so. Throughout her political career, Chisholm fought for education opportunities and social justice. Chisholm left Congress in 1983 to teach. First African-American Congresswoman. Chisholm became one of the founding members of the Congressional Black Caucus in 1969, and championed minority education and employment opportunities throughout her tenure in Congress.

Shirley Chisholm

Sidney Poitier

Sir Sidney Poitier, KBE is a Bahamian-American actor, film director, author, and diplomat. In 1964, Poitier became the first Bahamian and first black actor to win an Academy Award for Best Actor, and the Golden Globe Award for Best Actor for his role in Lilies of the Field. The significance of these achievements was bolstered in 1967, when he starred in three successful films, all of which dealt with issues involving race and race relations: To Sir, with Love; In the Heat of the Night; and Guess Who's Coming to Dinner, making him the top box-office star of that year. In 1999, the American Film Institute named Poitier among the Greatest Male Stars of classic Hollywood cinema, ranking 22nd on the list of 25.

Shelton Jackson "Spike" Lee is an American film director, producer, writer, and actor. His production company, 40 Acres and a Mule Filmworks, has produced over 35 films since 1983. Shelton Jackson "Spike" Lee (born March 20, 1957) is an American film director, producer, writer, and actor. He made his directorial debut with She's Gotta Have It (1986), and has since directed such films as Do the Right Thing (1989), Jungle Fever (1991), Malcolm X (1992), He Got Game (1998), The Original Kings of Comedy (2000), 25th Hour (2002), Inside Man (2006), Chi-Raq (2015), and BlacKkKlansman (2018). Lee also had starring roles in ten of his own films. Lee's films have examined race relations, colorism in the black community, the role of media in contemporary life, urban crime and poverty, and other political issues. He has won numerous accolades for his work, including an Academy Award for Best Adapted Screenplay, a Student Academy Award, a BAFTA Award for Best Adapted Screenplay, two Emmy Awards, two Peabody Awards, and the Cannes Grand Prix. He has also received an Academy Honorary Award, an Honorary BAFTA Award, an Honorary César, and the Dorothy and Lillian Gish Prize. In 2019 Spike wins his first competitive Oscar for "Black Klansman"

Lincoln Theodore Monroe Andrew Perry, better known by the stage name Stepin Fetchit, was an American vaudevillian, comedian and film actor, of Jamaican descent, considered to be the first black actor to have a successful film career. his greatest fame was throughout the 1930s. In films and on stage, the persona of Stepin Fetchit was billed as "the Laziest Man in the World".

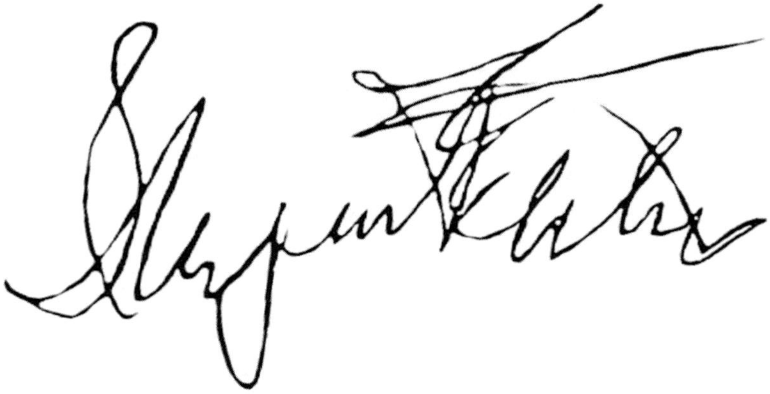

Stevie Wonder

Stevland Hardaway Morris, known by his stage name Stevie Wonder, is an American singer, songwriter, record producer, and multi- instrumentalist. A child prodigy, he is considered to be one of the most critically and commercially successful musical performers of the late 20th century. Wonder signed with Motown's Tamla label at the age of 11, and he continued performing and recording for Motown into the 2010s. He has been blind since shortly after birth.

Steve Wreeler

X

Thelonious Sphere Monk was an American jazz pianist and composer. He had a unique improvisational style and made numerous contributions to the standard jazz repertoire, including "'Round Midnight", "Blue Monk", "Straight, No Chaser", "Ruby, My Dear", "In Walked Bud", and "Well, You Needn't". Monk is the second-most-recorded jazz composer after Duke Ellington, which is particularly remarkable as Ellington composed more than a thousand pieces, whereas Monk wrote about 70.

Good luck
always

Thurgood Marshall

Thurgood Marshall was an American lawyer, serving as Associate Justice of the Supreme Court of the United States from October 1967 until October 1991. Marshall was the Court's 96th justice and its first African-American justice. Prior to his judicial service, he successfully argued several cases before the Supreme Court.

Thurgood Marshall

Eldrick Tont Woods (born December 30, 1975) better known as Tiger Woods, is an American professional golfer who is among the most successful golfers of all time. He has been one of the highest-paid athletes in the world for several years. Following an outstanding junior, college, and amateur career, Woods was 20 years old when he turned professional at the end of summer in 1996. By the end of April 1997, he had won three PGA Tour events in addition to his first major, the 1997 Masters. Woods won this tournament by 12 strokes in a record-breaking performance and earned $486,000. He first reached the number one position in the world rankings in June 1997, less than a year after turning pro. He was the top-ranked golfer in the world from August 1999 to September 2004 (264 weeks) and again from June 2005 to October 2010.

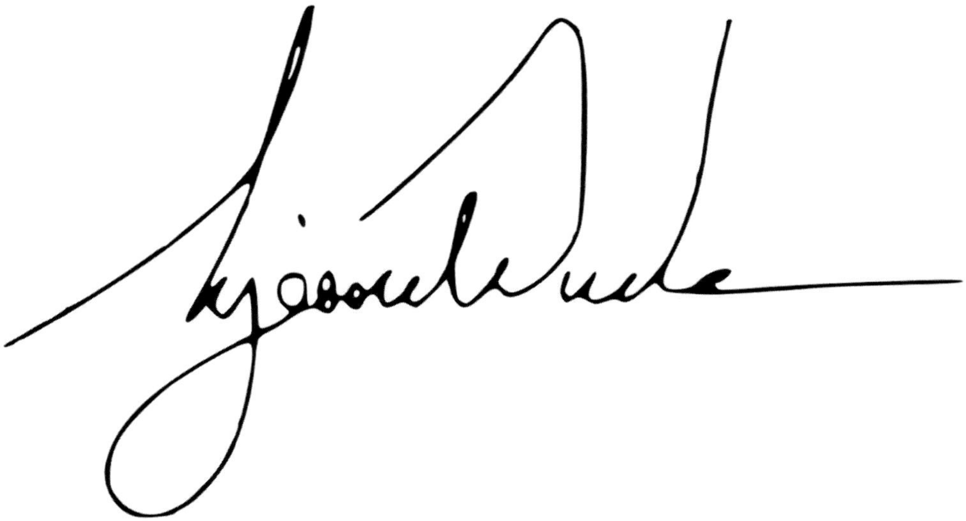

Tupac Amaru Shakur, also known by his stage names Tupac, 2Pac and Makaveli, was an American rapper and actor. Shakur sold over 75 million records world-wide, making him one of the best-selling music artists of all time. His double-disc albums All Eyez on Me and his Greatest Hits are among the best-selling albums in the United States. Shakur is consistently ranked as one of the greatest and most influential rappers of all time, and he has been listed and ranked as one of the greatest artists of any genre by many publications, including Rolling Stone, which ranked him 86th on its list of The 100 Greatest Artists of All Time. On April 7, 2017, Shakur was inducted into the Rock and Roll Hall of Fame in his first year of eligibility.

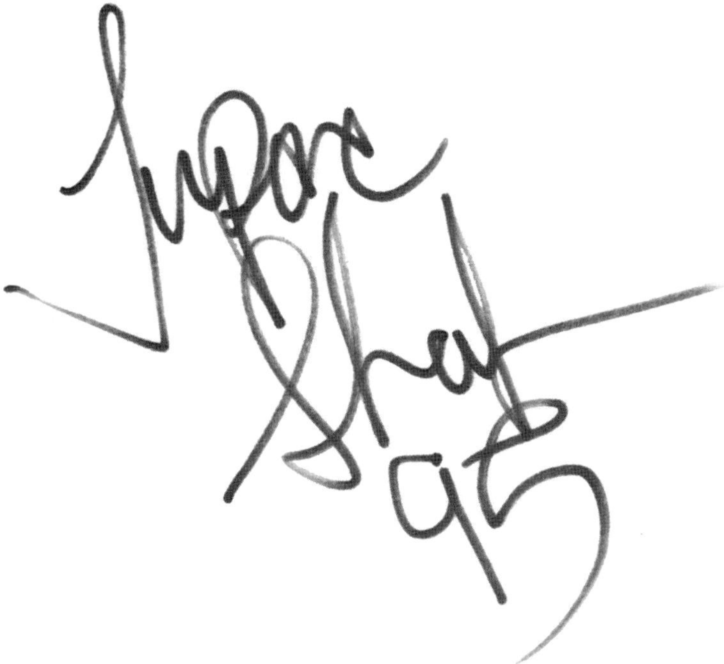

Venus Williams

Venus Ebony Starr Williams (born June 17, 1980) is an American professional tennis player who is currently ranked world No.16 in the WTA singles rankings. She is generally regarded as one of the all-time greats of women's tennis and, along with younger sister Serena Williams, is credited with ushering in a new era of power and athleticism on the women's professional tennis tour.

Williams has been ranked world No. 1 by the Women's Tennis Association on three occasions, for a total of 11 weeks. She first reached the No. 1 ranking on February 25, 2002, the first African American woman to do so in the Open Era, and the second all time since Althea Gibson. Williams' seven Grand Slam singles titles are tied for 12th on the all-time list, and 8th on the Open Era list, more than any other active female player except Serena. She has reached 16 Grand Slam finals, most recently at Wimbledon in 2017. She has also won 14 Grand Slam Women's doubles titles, all with Serena; the pair are unbeaten in Grand Slam doubles finals.

William Edward Burghardt "W. E. B." Du Bois was an American sociologist, historian, civil rights activist, Pan-Africanist, author, writer and editor. Born in Great Barrington, Massachusetts, Du Bois grew up in a relatively tolerant and integrated community. After completing graduate work at the University of Berlin and Harvard, where he was the first African American to earn a doctorate, he became a professor of history, sociology and economics at Atlanta University. Du Bois was one of the co-founders of the National Association for the Advancement of Colored People in 1909.

Whitney Houston

Whitney Elizabeth Houston was an American singer, actress, producer, and model. In 2009, Guinness World Records cited her as the most awarded female act of all time. Houston is one of the best-selling music artists of all-time, with 200 million records sold worldwide. She released seven studio albums and two soundtrack albums, all of which have diamond, multi-platinum, platinum, or gold certification. Houston's crossover appeal on the popular music charts--as well as her prominence on MTV, starting with her video for "How Will I Know"--influenced several African-American women artists who followed in her footsteps.

Will Smith

Willard Carroll Smith Jr. (born September 25, 1968) is an American actor, producer, comedian, rapper and songwriter. In April 2007, Newsweek called him "the most powerful actor in Hollywood". Smith has been nominated for five Golden Globe Awards and two Academy Awards, and has won four Grammy Awards. In the late 1980s, Smith achieved modest fame as a rapper under the name The Fresh Prince. In 1990, his popularity increased dramatically when he starred in the NBC television series The Fresh Prince of Bel-Air, which ran for six seasons until 1996. After the series ended, Smith transitioned from television to film, and has gone on to star in numerous blockbuster films. He is the only actor to have eight consecutive films gross over $100 million in the domestic box office, eleven consecutive films gross over $150 million internationally, and eight consecutive films in which he starred, open at the number one spot in the domestic box office tally. Smith has been ranked as the most bankable star worldwide by Forbes. As of 2014, 17 of the 21 films in which he has had leading roles have accumulated worldwide gross earnings of over $100 million each, five taking in over $500 million each in global box office receipts. As of 2016, his films have grossed $7.5 billion at the global box office. For his performances as boxer Muhammad Ali in Ali (2001) and stockbroker Chris Gardner in The Pursuit of Happyness (2006), Smith received nominations for the Academy Award for Best Actor.

Winnie Mandela

Winnie Madikizela-Mandela OLS, also known as Winnie Mandela, was a South African anti-apartheid activist and politician, and the ex-wife of Nelson Mandela. She served as a Member of Parliament from 1994 to 2003, and from 2009 until her death, and was a deputy minister from 1994 to 1996. A member of the African National Congress political party, she served on the ANC's National Executive Committee and headed its Women's League. Madikizela-Mandela was known to her supporters as the "Mother of the Nation".

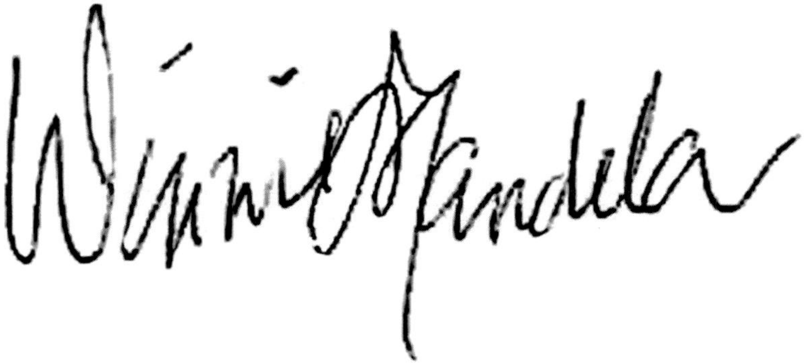
Winnie Mandela

Wynton Marsallis

Wynton Learson Marsalis is an American trumpeter, composer, teacher, and artistic director of Jazz at Lincoln Center. He has promoted classical and jazz music often to young audiences. Marsalis has been awarded nine Grammy Awards and his Blood on the Fields was the first jazz composition to win the Pulitzer Prize for Music. He is the son of jazz musician Ellis Marsalis Jr., grandson of Ellis Marsalis Sr., and brother of Branford, Delfeayo, and Jason. Marsalis is the only musician to win a Grammy Award in jazz and classical during the same year.

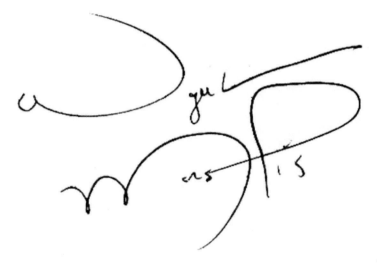

Sharad Davis / Rubin Bashir

My grandchildren are the inspiration and motivation for this book. Watching them go from infancy to school age and developing skills like reading and writing, brought back the times in my past when I was trying to learn how to write my name in cursive script. The first time I completed my full name as taught in grade school brought me great pride. So I can only imagine what it must have been for our slave ancestors to be denied such a blessing. We sometimes take the most common accomplishments like reading and writing for granted. But lets not forget that there once was a time not so long ago that it was against the law to teach slaves how to read or write.

So I ask, "Which of the favours of your Lord would you deny."

Sharad Davis

Grandson age 6 years

Author of "Signature"

Resources

Individual Photographs contained in this book are the copyright of the photographers and the intellectual property of each photographer. First Impressions does not claim any rights

Individual Biographies contained in this book are the copyright of **Wikipedia** (The Free Encyclopedia) and the text used was made available under the Creative Commons Attribution - ShareALike License: additional terms may apply. **Wikipedia** is a registered trademark of the Wilimedia Foundation, Inc. First Impressions does not claim any intellectual rights to any biographies found in this book.

Signatures contained in this book are the facsimiles of persons listed in this book, and was collected from items found in Public Domain (the state of belonging or being available to the public as a whole, and therefore not subject to copyright).

All signatures shown in this book were obtained from the following sources:
Photo Autographs, Signed Documents, Memorabilia Items, Sports Cards, and various
Autograph Websites, Autograph World.com • History For Sale.com, and
Direct request from individual listed participating celebrities.

Fountain Pen Photo on front cover and page 2 "Montblanc 82 fountain Pen is the copyright of Montblanc International writing instruments company.

All reasonable effort has been made to find and contact the copyright owners of the photographs printed in this publication. Any omissions or errors are inadvertent.

www.firstimpressionsbooks.com
ISBN: 978 1737709213
Library of Congress Control Number: 2018968318